Copyright © 2023 by Daniel W. Marshall (Author)

All rights reserved. This book or any portion thereof may not be reproduced or used in any manner whatsoever without the express written permission of the publisher except for the use of brief quotations in a book review.

This book is copyright protected. This is only for personal use. You cannot amend, distributor, sell, use, quote or paraphrase any part or the content within this book without the consent of the author.

Please note the information contained within this document is for educational and entertainment purposes only. Every attempt has been made to provide accurate, up to date and reliable complete information. No warranties of any kind are expressed or implied. Readers acknowledge that the author is not engaging in the rendering of legal, financial, medical or professional advice. The content of this book has been derived from various sources. Please consult a licensed professional before attempting any techniques outlined in this book.

By reading this document, the readers agree that under no circumstances are the author responsible for any losses, direct or indirect, which are incurred as a result of the use of information contained within this document, including but not limited to errors, omissions or inaccuracies.

Thank you very much for reading this book.

Title: Empowering a Unified Blockchain Future: Bridging the Gaps with Trustless Interoperability and Chain Keys
Subtitle: Enabling Seamless Crypto Communication: Paving the Way for a Connected Tokenized Economy

Author: Daniel W. Marshall

Table of Contents

Introduction **6**
The Dawn of Interoperability in the Blockchain Era 6
The Roadblocks to Seamless Communication 10
Unveiling the Path to Trustless Interoperability 14

Chapter 1: Delving into the World of Chain Keys ... **18**
The Essence of Trustless Communication 18
The Security Advantages of Chain Keys 22
The Pitfalls of Trustless Interoperability 27
Evaluating the Maturity of Chain Key Technology 33
Exploring Future Advancements in Chain Key Design 39

Chapter 2: Bridges: Bridging the Gaps between Blockchains **46**
The Architecture of Blockchain Bridges 46
The Role of Oracles and Relayers 57
The Pitfalls of Bridge-Based Interoperability 68
Evaluating the Security and Reliability of Bridges 81
Exploring Future Directions in Bridge Design 92

Chapter 3: A Comparative Analysis of Interoperability Approaches **103**
Chain Keys vs. Bridges: A Comprehensive Comparison .. 103
Evaluating the Pros and Cons of Chain Keys 109
Evaluating the Pros and Cons of Bridges 115
Matching the Approach to the Use Case 121
Considering the Trade-offs between Security, Trustlessness, Scalability, and User Experience 127

Chapter 4: The Case for Trustless Interoperability 133
Making a Strong Case for the Trustless Paradigm 133
Eliminating Reliance on Trusted Third Parties 141
Addressing Potential Concerns Regarding Chain Keys ... 148
The Future of Trustless Interoperability and Its Impact on the Blockchain Ecosystem 155
Fostering Collaboration and Open-Source Development in Trustless Interoperability 161

Chapter 5: Real-World Applications and the Future Landscape 168
Chain Keys in Practice: Showcasing Real-World Implementations 168
The Impact of Chain Key Implementations on Interoperability 175
Navigating the Challenges and Opportunities in the Evolving Blockchain Landscape 183
Emerging Trends and Advancements in Chain Key Technology 189
Envisioning the Future of Interoperable Blockchain Ecosystems 196

Conclusion 204
The Key Takeaways: A Reiteration of Chain Keys' Advantages 204
The Significance of Interoperability in the Growth of Blockchain Technology 209

A Call to Action: Exploring and Contributing to the Advancement of Trustless Interoperability 216

The Role of Chain Keys in Shaping the Future of a Unified Blockchain Landscape..222

Glossary **228**

Potential References...**231**

Introduction
The Dawn of Interoperability in the Blockchain Era

The blockchain landscape has undergone a revolutionary transformation since its inception, marked by an unprecedented proliferation of diverse networks and platforms. As this decentralized ecosystem continues to expand, the need for seamless communication and interoperability among different blockchains becomes increasingly apparent. This chapter explores the evolution of interoperability, examining the pivotal moment when the blockchain era embraced the concept and the challenges that spurred the development of innovative solutions.

The Genesis of Interoperability

The journey towards interoperability can be traced back to the early days of blockchain technology. Initially, individual blockchains operated in silos, functioning autonomously with limited connectivity to external networks. Bitcoin, the pioneer of blockchain, focused on peer-to-peer transactions, laying the foundation for decentralized, transparent, and secure transactions. However, the siloed nature of early blockchains hindered their ability to communicate and share data seamlessly.

Recognizing the Limitations

As blockchain technology gained traction, developers and enthusiasts recognized the limitations posed by the lack of interoperability. The fragmented nature of the blockchain ecosystem presented challenges for users and developers alike. Transactions and data were confined within specific chains, limiting the potential for collaboration and synergy across the broader decentralized landscape.

The Need for Interconnectedness

The recognition of these limitations led to a paradigm shift in the perception of blockchain technology. The community began to acknowledge that the true potential of this revolutionary technology could only be realized through interconnectedness. Blockchain was not just about individual chains but about creating an interwoven network that could facilitate value transfer, data sharing, and collaborative innovation on a global scale.

Catalysts for Change

Several factors acted as catalysts for the shift towards interoperability. The growing demand for scalability, the desire to explore new use cases, and the realization that a single blockchain could not cater to the diverse needs of users and applications fueled the drive for interoperability. Developers, blockchain projects, and industry leaders started envisioning a future where different blockchains could seamlessly communicate, enabling a more efficient and versatile decentralized ecosystem.

Navigating the Early Challenges

The early attempts at achieving interoperability were met with challenges. Technical complexities, security concerns, and the absence of standardized protocols posed significant hurdles. However, these challenges became stepping stones for innovation. Developers and researchers delved into finding solutions that would not compromise the fundamental principles of decentralization, security, and transparency.

Emergence of Interoperability Solutions

The dawn of interoperability witnessed the emergence of various solutions aimed at bridging the gaps between disparate blockchains. Interoperability protocols, cross-chain communication frameworks, and novel consensus mechanisms began to take shape. These solutions sought to create a cohesive network where blockchains could interact seamlessly, sharing assets, data, and functionalities in a trustless environment.

Chain Keys: A Glimpse into Trustless Interoperability

Among the diverse approaches to interoperability, the concept of chain keys emerged as a beacon of trustless communication. Chain keys, with their focus on secure and decentralized key management, played a crucial role in shaping the trajectory of interoperability. This chapter will delve deeper into the essence of chain keys, their security advantages, and the role they play in fostering a trustless model of interoperability.

In the subsequent chapters, we will explore the world of chain keys, delve into the architecture of blockchain bridges, conduct a comparative analysis of interoperability approaches, make a compelling case for trustless interoperability, and finally, envision the real-world applications and the future landscape of a unified blockchain ecosystem. The journey through these chapters will illuminate the path toward a future where interoperability is not just a possibility but a foundational element of blockchain technology.

The Roadblocks to Seamless Communication

Seamless communication between blockchains has long been the Holy Grail of the decentralized world—a utopian vision where different networks effortlessly exchange information, assets, and functionality. However, this vision is not without its share of challenges and roadblocks. In this chapter, we will delve into the intricacies of achieving seamless communication in the blockchain era, exploring the hurdles that have impeded progress and the innovative solutions that have emerged in response.

The Siloed Nature of Blockchains

One of the fundamental roadblocks to seamless communication lies in the inherent siloed nature of blockchains. Each blockchain operates as an independent entity, maintaining its ledger, consensus mechanism, and smart contract functionalities. While this autonomy ensures security and decentralization, it creates a barrier to fluid communication between different chains. Transactions, data, and assets are confined within the boundaries of each blockchain, hindering the seamless transfer of value and information.

Divergent Architectures and Standards

The blockchain ecosystem is diverse, with various projects adopting different architectures, consensus mechanisms, and standards. This diversity, while fostering innovation, poses a significant challenge for interoperability. Blockchains may use different programming languages, consensus algorithms, and data structures, making it difficult to establish a common language for communication.

Achieving seamless interoperability requires addressing these divergent elements and establishing standardized protocols that can be universally adopted.

Scalability Concerns

As the popularity of blockchain technology grows, scalability becomes a pressing concern. The increasing number of transactions and the growing size of blockchain ledgers contribute to network congestion and slower transaction processing times. Scalability challenges exacerbate the difficulties of achieving seamless communication, especially when dealing with a high volume of cross-chain transactions. Solutions that enhance scalability without compromising security are crucial for overcoming this roadblock.

Security Implications

Blockchain is built on the principles of decentralization and security. However, ensuring the same level of security in cross-chain communication introduces complexities. The challenge lies in maintaining the integrity of transactions and data as they traverse different blockchains. Security vulnerabilities, such as the risk of double-spending or data manipulation, need to be addressed to establish trust in cross-chain transactions. Striking a balance between security and interoperability is a delicate task that requires innovative cryptographic solutions and consensus mechanisms.

Lack of Standardized Interoperability Protocols

While several interoperability solutions have been proposed, the absence of standardized protocols has hindered widespread adoption. The lack of a universally accepted framework for cross-chain communication creates fragmentation and compatibility issues. Developers and blockchain projects often find themselves navigating a landscape of competing interoperability standards, making it challenging to implement seamless communication between blockchains. Establishing standardized protocols is essential for fostering collaboration and creating a cohesive blockchain ecosystem.

Trust Issues and Centralization Concerns

Traditional interoperability solutions often involve the use of intermediaries or trusted third parties to facilitate cross-chain transactions. While these approaches may address some technical challenges, they introduce trust issues and centralization concerns. Relying on intermediaries contradicts the decentralized ethos of blockchain technology and exposes users to the risk of censorship or manipulation. Overcoming trust issues is paramount for achieving seamless communication without compromising the core principles of decentralization and trustlessness.

Overcoming Roadblocks with Innovative Solutions

The roadblocks to seamless communication are formidable, but the blockchain community has not been idle in the face of these challenges. Innovative solutions, ranging from advanced cryptographic techniques to novel consensus mechanisms, are reshaping the landscape of interoperability. In the chapters that follow, we will explore these solutions in detail, with a particular focus on the role of chain keys and bridges in overcoming roadblocks and fostering a trustless model of interoperability.

The journey to seamless communication in the blockchain era is complex, but it is also a testament to the resilience and ingenuity of the blockchain community. By addressing these roadblocks head-on, we pave the way for a future where interoperability is not only achievable but forms the backbone of a unified and collaborative decentralized ecosystem.

Unveiling the Path to Trustless Interoperability

In the vast landscape of blockchain technology, the quest for trustless interoperability stands as a defining challenge and a beacon of innovation. As the blockchain ecosystem continues to evolve, the need for seamless communication between disparate networks becomes increasingly apparent. In this chapter, we embark on a journey to unveil the path to trustless interoperability, exploring the principles, technologies, and advancements that pave the way for a decentralized future where different blockchains can communicate without relying on intermediaries or compromising security.

The Foundation of Trustless Interoperability

At the core of trustless interoperability lies a fundamental shift in the way blockchains communicate. Unlike traditional approaches that rely on trusted intermediaries, trustless interoperability aims to establish direct and secure communication channels between blockchains. This paradigm shift is rooted in the principles of decentralization, transparency, and cryptographic security, ensuring that interactions between blockchains are verifiable, tamper-resistant, and free from the need for intermediaries.

Chain Keys: A Key Element in Trustless Interoperability

Chain keys emerge as a crucial element in the journey towards trustless interoperability. These cryptographic keys, intricately linked to the security and integrity of blockchain networks, provide a means for establishing trustless communication. Unlike traditional private keys that may rely on centralized entities for verification, chain keys are designed to operate in a decentralized environment, eliminating the need for trust in third parties. As we delve into the world of chain keys, we uncover their role in securing cross-chain transactions and enabling a trustless model of interoperability.

Decentralized Key Management

Trustless interoperability hinges on decentralized key management, a paradigm that empowers users with control over their private keys without relying on external entities. Decentralized key management ensures that users retain sovereignty over their assets and data, even when engaging in cross-chain transactions. The exploration of this decentralized key management paradigm unveils its significance in eliminating single points of failure and enhancing the security of blockchain interactions.

Smart Contracts as Enablers of Trustless Interaction

Smart contracts, the self-executing contracts with the terms of the agreement directly written into code, play a pivotal role in the path to trustless interoperability. These programmable scripts facilitate and automate the execution of cross-chain transactions without the need for intermediaries. By exploring the capabilities of smart contracts in ensuring trustless interactions, we uncover how they contribute to the efficiency, transparency, and security of cross-chain communication.

Bridging the Gap: The Role of Chain Bridges

While chain keys provide a foundation for trustless interoperability, the concept of chain bridges serves as a bridge between different blockchains, enabling them to communicate seamlessly. Chain bridges operate as decentralized connectors, facilitating the secure transfer of assets and data between disparate networks. Examining the architecture and functionality of chain bridges, we unveil how they contribute to the establishment of trustless communication and bridge the gaps that once hindered interoperability.

Overcoming Challenges with Trustless Approaches

Trustless interoperability is not without its challenges, and as we unveil the path forward, it is essential to address the hurdles that may arise. From potential security vulnerabilities to scalability concerns, understanding the challenges associated with trustless approaches allows us to develop robust solutions. By exploring how innovations such as advanced cryptographic techniques and consensus mechanisms contribute to overcoming these challenges, we gain insights into the resilience of trustless interoperability.

The Maturity of Trustless Interoperability Technologies

As we progress along the path to trustless interoperability, it is crucial to evaluate the maturity of the technologies that underpin this paradigm shift. Assessing the current state of chain key technology, decentralized key management, and chain bridges provides a comprehensive understanding of the advancements that have been made and the areas that continue to evolve. This exploration lays the groundwork for anticipating future developments and ensuring the continued growth of trustless interoperability.

A Glimpse into the Future

The journey to trustless interoperability extends beyond the current landscape, offering a glimpse into the future of decentralized communication. By examining emerging trends, ongoing research, and the collaborative efforts within the blockchain community, we gain foresight into the potential advancements that will shape the future of trustless interoperability. This forward-looking perspective serves as an inspiration for developers, researchers, and enthusiasts who are committed to building a decentralized future.

In the subsequent chapters, we will delve into the world of chain keys, explore the architecture of blockchain bridges, conduct a comparative analysis of interoperability approaches, make a compelling case for trustless interoperability, showcase real-world applications, and envision the future landscape of a unified blockchain ecosystem. The unveiling of the path to trustless interoperability sets the stage for a comprehensive exploration of the technologies and principles that drive the evolution of decentralized communication in the blockchain era.

Chapter 1: Delving into the World of Chain Keys

The Essence of Trustless Communication

In the intricate web of blockchain technology, the concept of trustless communication stands as a cornerstone, reshaping the way different blockchain networks interact. As we delve into the world of chain keys in this chapter, we unravel the essence of trustless communication— a paradigm that eliminates reliance on intermediaries, fosters transparency, and ensures the security of transactions across decentralized networks.

Redefining Trust in the Blockchain Era

The traditional notion of trust, often rooted in centralized authorities, undergoes a transformation within the blockchain era. Trustless communication fundamentally redefines how trust is established and maintained in the digital realm. Rather than relying on trusted third parties or intermediaries to facilitate transactions, blockchain technology leverages cryptographic principles to enable verifiable and tamper-resistant interactions between parties who may have no pre-existing trust.

The Role of Chain Keys in Trustless Communication

At the heart of trustless communication lies the concept of chain keys. These cryptographic keys, intricately tied to the security and integrity of blockchain networks, play a pivotal role in establishing and verifying the identity of participants in a transaction. Unlike traditional public-private key pairs, chain keys are designed to operate within a decentralized environment, enabling users to engage in transactions without the need for a trusted intermediary.

Understanding the mechanics of chain keys allows us to appreciate how they form the bedrock of trustless communication.

Decentralized Key Management: Empowering Users

Trustless communication is closely intertwined with the concept of decentralized key management. In a decentralized ecosystem, users maintain control over their private keys, eliminating the need to trust third-party entities with custodial responsibilities. This shift towards decentralized key management empowers users with greater autonomy and control over their assets and data. As we explore the essence of decentralized key management, we gain insights into how it strengthens the security and trustlessness of blockchain transactions.

Verifiability and Transparency

Trustless communication places a premium on verifiability and transparency. Every transaction conducted within a trustless framework is verifiable by all participants in the network. The transparent nature of blockchain ledgers ensures that the details of transactions, from initiation to completion, are visible to anyone who wishes to scrutinize them. This transparency fosters a sense of accountability and trust among users, as they can independently verify the validity and authenticity of transactions.

Smart Contracts: Executing Trustless Agreements

Smart contracts further amplify the essence of trustless communication by automating and self-executing agreements without the need for intermediaries. These programmable scripts encode the terms and conditions of an agreement, ensuring that the agreed-upon actions are executed automatically when predefined conditions are met. Trustless smart contracts eliminate the need to rely on external parties to enforce agreements, providing a level of trust and efficiency previously unattainable in traditional contractual arrangements.

Immutable Record-Keeping

The trustless nature of blockchain communication is reinforced by the immutability of the underlying ledger. Once a transaction is recorded on the blockchain, it becomes a permanent part of the historical record. This immutability ensures that transactions cannot be altered or tampered with retrospectively. The unchangeable nature of the blockchain ledger adds an extra layer of trust to the communication process, as participants can have confidence that the historical record is incorruptible.

Eliminating Counterparty Risk

Trustless communication addresses the issue of counterparty risk inherent in traditional financial transactions. In a trustless environment, participants can engage in transactions with one another without relying on a central authority to guarantee the fulfillment of obligations. The use of cryptographic keys, smart contracts, and transparent ledgers ensures that parties can transact directly with one another, reducing the need for trust in the reliability and integrity of their counterparties.

Resilience to Single Points of Failure

The essence of trustless communication is closely linked to the resilience of the blockchain network to single points of failure. Traditional systems often rely on centralized entities, creating vulnerabilities where a single failure could disrupt the entire network. In a trustless blockchain environment, the absence of central points of control distributes the responsibility and risk across the network, making it more robust and resistant to systemic failures.

Challenges and Solutions in Trustless Communication

While trustless communication offers groundbreaking advantages, it is not without challenges. Addressing potential security vulnerabilities, ensuring scalability, and navigating regulatory landscapes are among the hurdles that need to be overcome. However, innovative solutions, ranging from advanced cryptographic techniques to consensus mechanisms, are continually being developed to enhance the trustlessness of blockchain communication.

In the subsequent sections of this chapter, we will explore the security advantages of chain keys, evaluate the pitfalls of trustless interoperability, assess the maturity of chain key technology, and glimpse into the future advancements in chain key design. As we unravel the intricacies of chain keys, the essence of trustless communication will continue to guide our understanding of how blockchain technology transforms the way we communicate and transact in a decentralized world.

The Security Advantages of Chain Keys

In the dynamic landscape of blockchain technology, security is paramount. As we delve into the world of chain keys, a critical element of trustless communication, we uncover the multifaceted security advantages that these cryptographic keys bring to the forefront. From protecting user identities to securing the integrity of transactions, chain keys play a pivotal role in fortifying the robustness of blockchain networks.

Immutable Identity Verification

Chain keys serve as the immutable digital identities of participants in a blockchain network. Unlike traditional authentication methods that may rely on centralized authorities, chain keys offer a decentralized and tamper-resistant approach to identity verification. The cryptographic nature of chain keys ensures that once an identity is established, it remains unchanged and cannot be forged or manipulated. This immutability adds an extra layer of security to user authentication, reducing the risk of identity-related fraud and ensuring the integrity of participant identities within the blockchain ecosystem.

Private Key Security

One of the foundational principles of blockchain security is the safeguarding of private keys. In the context of chain keys, the security of private keys is of utmost importance. Private keys are used to sign transactions, providing cryptographic proof of the owner's authorization. The decentralized nature of blockchain networks, coupled with the cryptographic strength of private keys, enhances the security of user accounts. Chain keys empower users with control over their private keys, reducing the risk of unauthorized access or compromise.

Trustless Transactions and Counterparty Risk Mitigation

Chain keys contribute significantly to the security of transactions by facilitating trustless interactions. In a trustless environment, participants can engage in transactions without relying on trusted intermediaries. The cryptographic signatures generated by chain keys serve as proof of authorization, enabling secure and verifiable transactions. This trustless model reduces counterparty risk, as participants can transact directly with one another without the need for a central authority to ensure the fulfillment of obligations. The security advantage lies in the elimination of reliance on third parties, fostering a more resilient and efficient transactional framework.

Resilience to Sybil Attacks

Sybil attacks, wherein a malicious actor creates multiple fake identities to gain control over a network, are a persistent concern in decentralized systems. Chain keys play a crucial role in mitigating the risk of Sybil attacks by requiring a unique cryptographic key for each participant. Each chain key serves as a distinct digital identity, making it computationally infeasible for a single actor to generate a multitude of valid identities. The cryptographic uniqueness of chain keys enhances the resilience of blockchain networks against Sybil attacks, bolstering the overall security of the system.

Non-Repudiation and Transaction Integrity

Non-repudiation, the inability of a participant to deny the authenticity of their actions, is a fundamental security principle in blockchain transactions. Chain keys, through the use of cryptographic signatures, provide a mechanism for non-repudiation. When a participant signs a transaction with their private key, the cryptographic signature serves as irrefutable proof of their involvement. This non-repudiation feature ensures the integrity of transactions, preventing participants from denying their actions after the fact. The security advantage lies in the ability to establish a trustworthy and unforgeable record of transactions.

Privacy and Anonymity Features

While the transparency of blockchain ledgers is a key strength, privacy considerations are also vital. Chain keys contribute to privacy and anonymity by allowing users to transact without revealing their real-world identities. The cryptographic nature of chain keys enables pseudonymous interactions, wherein users are identified by their unique cryptographic keys rather than personal information. This privacy feature enhances the security of user identities by minimizing the exposure of sensitive information, fostering a more secure and discreet transactional environment.

Protection Against Replay Attacks

Replay attacks involve malicious actors intercepting and retransmitting valid transactions to deceive the network. Chain keys enhance security by incorporating mechanisms to protect against replay attacks. Each transaction, when signed with a chain key, includes a timestamp and unique transaction information. This information, combined with cryptographic hashing, ensures that each transaction is unique and cannot be reused in a replay attack. The security advantage lies in the prevention of unauthorized reuse of valid transactions, safeguarding the integrity of the blockchain network.

Smart Contract Security

In the context of smart contracts, chain keys play a vital role in ensuring the security of contract execution. Smart contracts are self-executing agreements that rely on predefined conditions and cryptographic signatures for execution. Chain keys associated with smart contracts contribute to the security of these agreements by requiring cryptographic proof of authorization. This security feature ensures that only authorized parties can interact with and execute smart contracts, reducing the risk of unauthorized access or manipulation.

Interoperability and Cross-Chain Security

As the blockchain ecosystem evolves, interoperability between different chains becomes a focal point. Chain keys contribute to the security of cross-chain transactions by providing a standardized and secure method for identity verification. The use of chain keys in cross-chain communication ensures that participants from different networks can securely transact without compromising the security of their respective chains. This interoperability feature enhances the overall security of the blockchain ecosystem by enabling secure interactions between diverse networks.

Challenges and Ongoing Innovations in Chain Key Security

While chain keys offer a myriad of security advantages, challenges such as quantum computing threats, key management complexities, and potential vulnerabilities still need to be addressed. Ongoing research and innovations in cryptographic techniques, key management protocols, and quantum-resistant algorithms are at the forefront of enhancing the security of chain keys. Understanding these challenges and the evolving landscape of security innovations is crucial for maintaining the robustness of chain key-based security frameworks.

In the subsequent sections of this chapter, we will further explore the pitfalls of trustless interoperability, evaluate the maturity of chain key technology, and delve into the future advancements in chain key design. As we uncover the security advantages of chain keys, the intricate interplay between cryptographic principles and decentralized identity management emerges as a foundational element in fortifying the security posture of blockchain networks.

The Pitfalls of Trustless Interoperability

As we navigate the intricate landscape of blockchain technology and delve into the world of chain keys, it is essential to acknowledge the challenges and pitfalls that accompany the pursuit of trustless interoperability. While trustless communication holds the promise of decentralized, secure interactions, several hurdles and complexities must be addressed to fully realize this vision. In this chapter, we explore the pitfalls of trustless interoperability, ranging from technical challenges to conceptual considerations, shedding light on the nuanced aspects that demand attention in the quest for seamless blockchain communication.

Complexity of Cross-Chain Communication

One of the primary pitfalls of trustless interoperability is the inherent complexity of cross-chain communication. Integrating different blockchains, each with its unique architecture, consensus mechanism, and data structure, poses significant technical challenges. Ensuring that chain keys and other trustless mechanisms work seamlessly across diverse networks requires meticulous attention to detail. Developers must grapple with the intricacies of varying protocols, smart contract languages, and transaction formats, making the process of achieving trustless interoperability inherently complex.

Scalability Concerns

Scalability remains a persistent challenge in the blockchain space, and trustless interoperability exacerbates this concern. As the number of interconnected blockchains and the volume of cross-chain transactions increase, the scalability of the entire ecosystem comes into question. The decentralized nature of blockchain networks, coupled with the computational requirements of trustless mechanisms, can lead to performance bottlenecks. Scalability challenges not only impact transaction throughput but also pose hurdles in maintaining the efficiency and responsiveness of interconnected networks.

Security Risks in Cross-Chain Transactions

While trustless mechanisms aim to enhance security, the execution of cross-chain transactions introduces new security considerations. The process of moving assets or data between blockchains inherently involves additional complexities and potential vulnerabilities. Issues such as atomicity, where transactions must either be completed in full or rolled back entirely, and the risk of front-running attacks require meticulous attention to detail. Trustless interoperability solutions must rigorously address these security risks to maintain the integrity and confidentiality of cross-chain transactions.

Consensus Divergence

Divergence in consensus mechanisms among interconnected blockchains poses a substantial challenge to trustless interoperability. Blockchains may employ different consensus algorithms, such as proof-of-work (PoW), proof-of-stake (PoS), or delegated proof-of-stake (DPoS). Achieving consensus across heterogeneous networks introduces complexities in ensuring a consistent understanding of transaction finality and validation. Overcoming consensus divergence is crucial for trustless interoperability, as it directly impacts the reliability and security of cross-chain transactions.

Standardization and Interoperability Protocols

The absence of standardized protocols for trustless interoperability is a significant hurdle. Without universally accepted standards, developers face the challenge of creating solutions that can seamlessly integrate with a diverse range of blockchains. The lack of standardized interfaces and protocols can lead to fragmentation, interoperability issues, and hinder widespread adoption. Establishing common standards is essential for fostering collaboration and ensuring that trustless interoperability solutions can be universally implemented across the blockchain ecosystem.

Key Management and User Experience

While chain keys contribute to the security of trustless interoperability, they also introduce challenges related to key management and user experience. Users must securely manage their private keys to maintain control over their assets and identities. The responsibility of key management can be daunting for non-technical users, potentially leading to the risk of lost keys or unauthorized access. Balancing security with user-friendly key management solutions is crucial for ensuring the widespread adoption and usability of trustless interoperability.

Quantum Computing Threats

The advent of quantum computing poses a looming threat to the security of existing cryptographic algorithms, including those used in trustless interoperability solutions. Quantum computers have the potential to break widely used encryption methods, compromising the security of private keys and transactions. Preparing for the era of quantum computing is imperative for trustless interoperability, requiring the development and adoption of quantum-resistant cryptographic techniques to safeguard against future threats.

Regulatory Challenges

Trustless interoperability operates in a regulatory landscape that is still evolving. Regulatory uncertainty can create challenges for the adoption and implementation of trustless solutions, especially when dealing with cross-border transactions and compliance requirements. Navigating regulatory frameworks, ensuring compliance with data protection laws, and addressing concerns related to privacy and identity verification are integral aspects that must be considered to achieve trustless interoperability on a global scale.

Decentralization vs. Centralization Dilemma

While trustless interoperability aims to maintain the principles of decentralization, some solutions may inadvertently introduce elements of centralization. The use of oracles or relayers to facilitate cross-chain communication, for example, can become potential points of centralization. Striking the right balance between decentralization and the practicalities of efficient cross-chain communication is a nuanced challenge that requires careful consideration in the design and implementation of trustless interoperability solutions.

Governance and Decision-Making

The governance of trustless interoperability networks presents its own set of challenges. Decentralized networks often rely on governance models to make decisions regarding upgrades, protocol changes, and dispute resolution. Achieving consensus in a decentralized manner while avoiding governance-related disputes is a complex task. Navigating the governance challenges of trustless interoperability networks requires transparent and inclusive decision-making processes that align with the decentralized ethos of blockchain technology.

Education and User Awareness

The success of trustless interoperability solutions hinges on user adoption and understanding. Educating users about the benefits, risks, and functionalities of trustless interoperability is crucial for fostering widespread adoption. Lack of awareness or misunderstanding of the intricacies of trustless mechanisms can lead to user errors, security vulnerabilities, and hinder the overall success of interoperability initiatives. Bridging the gap between technical complexity and user-friendly interfaces is a challenge that must be addressed to ensure the seamless integration of trustless interoperability into the broader blockchain ecosystem.

In the subsequent sections of this chapter, we will explore the maturity of chain key technology, delve into the architecture of blockchain bridges, conduct a comparative analysis of interoperability approaches, and make a compelling case for trustless interoperability. By acknowledging and addressing these pitfalls, we pave the way for a more robust and resilient trustless interoperability framework that aligns with the core principles of blockchain technology.

Evaluating the Maturity of Chain Key Technology

As we embark on an exploration of the world of chain keys, a critical aspect that demands attention is the maturity of the underlying technology. Chain keys, serving as the cryptographic linchpin for trustless communication and interoperability in blockchain networks, must demonstrate a level of maturity that instills confidence in their reliability, security, and practical applicability. In this chapter, we delve into the evaluation of the maturity of chain key technology, scrutinizing its evolution, current state, and the challenges and advancements that shape its trajectory within the dynamic landscape of blockchain innovation.

Evolution of Chain Key Technology

The evolution of chain key technology is deeply intertwined with the broader development of blockchain ecosystems. In the early stages of blockchain adoption, cryptographic key management primarily focused on traditional public and private key pairs for securing transactions. However, as the need for trustless communication and interoperability grew, the concept of chain keys emerged.

The notion of chain keys represents a shift towards decentralized key management, where users maintain control over their keys without relying on centralized entities. This evolution reflects a maturation of cryptographic principles within the blockchain space, aligning with the foundational tenets of decentralization, security, and user sovereignty.

Key Components of Chain Key Technology

To evaluate the maturity of chain key technology, it is essential to understand its key components. Chain keys typically consist of public and private key pairs, similar to traditional cryptographic key pairs. However, what sets chain keys apart is their integration into the decentralized fabric of blockchain networks. The public key serves as an identifier for users, while the private key, securely held by the user, is used to sign transactions and establish trustless communication.

As chain key technology matures, advancements may include improvements in key generation algorithms, enhanced cryptographic techniques, and innovations in key storage solutions. Evaluating these key components provides insights into the sophistication and resilience of chain key technology.

Security Advancements and Innovations

Security is a paramount concern in blockchain technology, and chain keys play a pivotal role in ensuring the integrity and confidentiality of transactions. Evaluating the maturity of chain key technology involves assessing the security advancements and innovations that have been integrated to address potential vulnerabilities.

Innovations in cryptographic techniques, such as zero-knowledge proofs and homomorphic encryption, contribute to enhancing the security of chain keys. These advancements aim to fortify the privacy, authenticity, and non-repudiation features of chain key-based transactions. Additionally, the exploration of post-quantum cryptographic algorithms becomes increasingly relevant, anticipating the future landscape of quantum-resistant chain key technology.

Standardization and Interoperability

The maturity of chain key technology is closely linked to standardization efforts within the blockchain space. Standardized protocols for key generation, storage, and communication contribute to the interoperability of chain keys across different blockchain networks. Efforts to establish common standards enable developers to create interoperable solutions that seamlessly integrate with diverse ecosystems.

The emergence of industry-wide initiatives and collaborative projects focused on standardizing chain key technology is indicative of its growing maturity. Evaluating the degree of standardization in chain key protocols provides a measure of the technology's readiness for widespread adoption and integration into the broader blockchain landscape.

Decentralized Key Management Solutions

Decentralized key management is a core principle of chain key technology, and the maturity of this aspect directly impacts user experience and security. As chain key technology evolves, the development of user-friendly decentralized key management solutions becomes crucial. User interfaces, recovery mechanisms, and educational resources all contribute to the usability and accessibility of chain keys.

Mature chain key technology should offer robust solutions for key management that cater to both technical and non-technical users. Evaluating the user experience and the effectiveness of decentralized key management solutions provides insights into the practical viability of chain keys in real-world applications.

Quantum-Resistant Approaches

The advent of quantum computing introduces a new dimension to the evaluation of chain key technology. As quantum computers pose a potential threat to traditional cryptographic algorithms, the maturity of chain key technology must encompass quantum-resistant approaches. Evaluating the integration of quantum-resistant cryptographic techniques into chain key protocols is crucial for ensuring the long-term security of blockchain networks.

Quantum-resistant chain key technology may involve the adoption of lattice-based cryptography, hash-based signatures, or other quantum-resistant algorithms. The proactive integration of such approaches signals the maturity of chain key technology in anticipating and mitigating emerging threats.

Real-World Implementations and Use Cases

One of the most tangible indicators of the maturity of chain key technology lies in its real-world implementations and use cases. Evaluating how chain keys are applied in practical scenarios provides valuable insights into their effectiveness, scalability, and adaptability to diverse applications.

Real-world implementations may span industries such as finance, healthcare, supply chain, and identity management. Assessing the success stories, challenges faced, and lessons learned from these implementations contributes to a comprehensive evaluation of chain key technology's maturity and its potential impact on various sectors.

Challenges and Ongoing Research

A mature technology acknowledges its challenges and actively engages in ongoing research to address them. Evaluating the maturity of chain key technology involves a critical examination of the existing challenges and the industry's response in terms of research and development efforts.

Key challenges may include issues related to key recovery, key revocation, quantum computing threats, and the scalability of decentralized key management solutions. Understanding how the blockchain community tackles these challenges provides valuable insights into the resilience and commitment to continuous improvement within the realm of chain key technology.

Collaboration and Open-Source Development

The collaborative nature of blockchain development and open-source initiatives is a hallmark of a mature technological ecosystem. Evaluating the level of collaboration and open-source contributions within the chain key technology space sheds light on the collective effort to advance the state of the technology.

Open-source projects focused on chain key technology, contributions to standardization bodies, and collaborative research endeavors all contribute to the maturity of the technology. The degree of community involvement and the existence of vibrant ecosystems around chain key technology signal its readiness for broader adoption and integration.

Future Roadmap and Upcoming Advancements

Finally, the evaluation of the maturity of chain key technology extends to its future roadmap and the anticipated advancements on the horizon. A mature technology is forward-looking, adapting to emerging trends and preparing for the challenges of tomorrow.

Exploring the roadmap of chain key technology may involve understanding planned upgrades, upcoming research initiatives, and collaborations with other emerging technologies such as decentralized identity solutions and secure multi-party computation. Evaluating the trajectory of chain key technology provides valuable insights into its continued relevance and potential impact on the future of blockchain ecosystems.

In the subsequent chapters, we will continue our exploration of chain keys, delving into the architecture of blockchain bridges, conducting a comparative analysis of interoperability approaches, making a compelling case for trustless interoperability, showcasing real-world applications, and envisioning the future landscape of a unified blockchain ecosystem. The evaluation of the maturity of chain key technology serves as a foundational step in understanding its role as a linchpin for trustless communication and interoperability in the ever-evolving world of blockchain innovation.

Exploring Future Advancements in Chain Key Design

As we delve into the intricate realm of chain keys, it is essential to cast our gaze forward and explore the future advancements that will shape the design and capabilities of these cryptographic entities. Chain keys, serving as the linchpin for trustless communication and interoperability in blockchain networks, are subject to continual innovation and evolution. In this chapter, we embark on a journey to anticipate and understand the potential future advancements in chain key design, examining the trends, challenges, and transformative possibilities that lie on the horizon.

Quantum-Resistant Chain Keys

One of the most pressing considerations for the future of chain key design is the looming threat posed by quantum computing. As quantum computers advance, traditional cryptographic algorithms may become vulnerable, potentially compromising the security of chain keys. Anticipating this challenge, the exploration of quantum-resistant chain key designs becomes paramount.

Future advancements in chain key design may involve the adoption of post-quantum cryptographic techniques, such as lattice-based cryptography, hash-based signatures, or multivariate polynomial cryptography. These quantum-resistant approaches aim to fortify chain keys against the cryptographic threats posed by quantum computers, ensuring the continued security of blockchain networks in an era of evolving technology.

Enhanced Privacy Features

Privacy is a fundamental concern in blockchain networks, and future advancements in chain key design will likely focus on enhancing privacy features. Current chain key systems offer pseudonymous interactions, but there is room for improvement in providing more robust privacy guarantees.

One potential avenue for advancement is the integration of advanced zero-knowledge proofs, such as zk-SNARKs (Zero-Knowledge Succinct Non-Interactive Arguments of Knowledge) or zk-STARKs (Zero-Knowledge Scalable Transparent Arguments of Knowledge). These privacy-centric cryptographic techniques could empower chain keys to facilitate transactions with even greater anonymity and confidentiality, addressing the demand for enhanced privacy in blockchain transactions.

Interoperability Standards

The future of chain key design is intricately linked to the broader landscape of blockchain interoperability. As blockchain ecosystems continue to expand and diversify, the development of interoperability standards for chain keys becomes essential. Standardized protocols can facilitate seamless communication between different blockchains, enabling chain keys to operate across various networks without the need for extensive modifications.

Advancements in chain key design may involve the establishment of industry-wide interoperability standards, defining common interfaces and communication protocols. This standardization would not only enhance the interoperability of chain keys but also contribute to the overall cohesion of the blockchain ecosystem.

Smart Contracts Integration

Smart contracts have become a cornerstone of blockchain technology, automating and self-executing contractual agreements. Future advancements in chain key design may explore deeper integration with smart contracts, unlocking new possibilities for programmable and trustless interactions.

Innovations could involve the development of chain key-specific smart contract languages or extensions that enable more complex and dynamic interactions. This integration could empower chain keys to participate seamlessly in a broader range of decentralized applications (DApps) and smart contract-based workflows, expanding their utility beyond simple transactional use cases.

Cross-Chain Communication Protocols

Cross-chain communication is a key challenge in blockchain interoperability, and future advancements in chain key design will likely focus on optimizing protocols for secure and efficient cross-chain transactions. Current approaches, such as sidechains and blockchain bridges, may evolve to become more streamlined and standardized.

Advanced cross-chain communication protocols could enhance the speed, security, and reliability of chain key interactions across different blockchains. These protocols might leverage concepts like atomic swaps, where assets can be exchanged across chains atomically, further strengthening the trustless nature of cross-chain transactions involving chain keys.

Decentralized Identity Solutions

Decentralized identity solutions are gaining prominence as blockchain technology matures, and future advancements in chain key design may contribute to the evolution of identity management. Chain keys could play a pivotal role in decentralized identity frameworks, serving as the cryptographic foundation for secure and self-sovereign identity verification.

The integration of chain keys with decentralized identity solutions could offer users greater control over their personal information, allowing them to selectively share identity attributes without compromising privacy. This advancement could find applications in areas such as identity verification for financial services, access control, and secure online interactions.

User-Friendly Key Management

As blockchain technology becomes more accessible to mainstream users, future advancements in chain key design will likely prioritize user-friendly key management solutions. Overcoming the challenges associated with secure key storage, backup, and recovery is crucial for ensuring widespread adoption and usability.

Innovations may involve the development of intuitive key management interfaces, seamless recovery mechanisms, and enhanced user education. Future chain key designs could prioritize a balance between robust security and a user-friendly experience, empowering a broader audience to participate in trustless communication and interoperability.

Integration with Emerging Technologies

The future of chain key design extends beyond blockchain technology alone. Integration with emerging technologies, such as decentralized finance (DeFi), artificial intelligence (AI), and the Internet of Things (IoT), holds the potential for transformative applications.

Chain keys could serve as the secure credentials for AI algorithms, enabling trustless interactions between decentralized AI agents. In the realm of DeFi, chain keys might facilitate automated and secure financial transactions. Integration with IoT devices could leverage chain keys for secure device identity and communication.

Continuous Research and Collaboration

Future advancements in chain key design will undoubtedly be fueled by continuous research and collaboration within the blockchain community. The open-source nature of blockchain development encourages collaboration, and ongoing research initiatives will shape the trajectory of chain key technology.

Research efforts may focus on addressing existing challenges, refining cryptographic algorithms, and exploring novel approaches to key management. Collaboration between industry stakeholders, academic institutions, and open-source communities will be instrumental in driving the innovation necessary for the continuous improvement of chain key technology.

Ethical and Regulatory Considerations

As chain key technology evolves, future advancements will need to navigate ethical and regulatory considerations. The integration of chain keys into various applications, especially those involving sensitive data or financial transactions, may raise ethical questions related to privacy, security, and user consent.

Future advancements in chain key design should proactively address ethical considerations and comply with emerging regulatory frameworks. Collaborative efforts between the blockchain industry, policymakers, and regulatory bodies will play a vital role in establishing ethical guidelines and ensuring the responsible development and deployment of chain key technology.

Conclusion

Exploring the future advancements in chain key design opens a window into the transformative possibilities that lie ahead for blockchain technology. From quantum-resistant security measures to enhanced privacy features, interoperability standards, and integration with emerging technologies, the future of chain keys holds promise for unlocking new dimensions of trustless communication and interoperability.

As we move forward in this exploration, subsequent chapters will delve into the architecture of blockchain bridges, conduct a comparative analysis of interoperability approaches, make a compelling case for trustless interoperability, showcase real-world applications, and envision the future landscape of a unified blockchain ecosystem. The anticipation of future advancements in chain key design underscores the dynamic and innovative nature of blockchain technology, setting the stage for a continued evolution towards more secure, efficient, and user-friendly blockchain ecosystems.

Chapter 2: Bridges: Bridging the Gaps between Blockchains

The Architecture of Blockchain Bridges

In the intricate landscape of blockchain technology, the concept of bridges emerges as a fundamental mechanism to facilitate interoperability and communication between disparate blockchain networks. As we embark on a journey to explore the bridges that bridge the gaps between blockchains, understanding the architecture of these crucial components becomes paramount. This chapter delves into the intricacies of the architecture of blockchain bridges, unraveling the layers, protocols, and technologies that enable the seamless flow of information and assets across decentralized networks.

Introduction to Blockchain Bridges

Blockchain bridges serve as connective tissue in the decentralized landscape, enabling the exchange of assets, data, and information between different blockchains. Their significance lies in mitigating the siloed nature of individual blockchain networks, fostering collaboration, and unlocking new possibilities for cross-chain interactions.

The architecture of blockchain bridges is designed to address the challenges posed by diverse consensus mechanisms, data structures, and smart contract languages that characterize various blockchains. By providing a standardized interface for communication, bridges facilitate trustless and secure transactions between otherwise isolated networks.

Key Components of Bridge Architecture

The architecture of blockchain bridges comprises several key components, each playing a crucial role in ensuring the reliability, security, and efficiency of cross-chain communication. Understanding these components sheds light on the complexity and sophistication of bridge design.

1. Oracle Networks

At the core of many blockchain bridges are oracle networks. Oracles act as data carriers, relaying information between different blockchains. They play a pivotal role in bridging the information asymmetry between blockchains, ensuring that each network has access to relevant and accurate data from the others.

The architecture involves a decentralized oracle network that retrieves and verifies data from one blockchain and broadcasts it to another. This process is crucial for executing smart contracts and transactions that rely on external data, such as price feeds, weather conditions, or real-world events.

2. Smart Contracts

Smart contracts are the executable code on blockchains that automate and enforce predefined rules. In the context of bridges, smart contracts play a central role in governing the cross-chain interactions. They define the conditions under which assets or information can be transferred from one blockchain to another.

The architecture of blockchain bridges involves the deployment of smart contracts that act as escrow agents, holding assets until predefined conditions are met. These contracts ensure the trustless nature of cross-chain transactions, as participants can be confident that the terms of the interaction will be automatically enforced.

3. Validators and Consensus Mechanism

Validators are nodes or entities responsible for validating transactions and ensuring the security and integrity of the bridge. The architecture often employs a consensus mechanism that aligns with the underlying blockchain's consensus model. For example, a bridge connecting a proof-of-work blockchain to a proof-of-stake blockchain may use a consensus algorithm that accommodates both models.

Validators participate in reaching a consensus on the validity of cross-chain transactions. Their role is crucial in preventing double-spending and ensuring that the state of each connected blockchain remains consistent.

4. Token Locking Mechanism

To facilitate the transfer of assets between blockchains, a token locking mechanism is employed in the architecture of blockchain bridges. This mechanism involves locking a certain amount of tokens on one blockchain to mint an equivalent amount on another. This ensures that the total supply of the asset remains constant, and the transfer is executed in a secure and verifiable manner.

The token locking mechanism is often implemented through the use of smart contracts, where tokens are escrowed until the conditions for unlocking on the destination blockchain are met.

5. Decentralized Identifiers (DIDs) and Chain Keys

Decentralized identifiers (DIDs) and chain keys play a role in ensuring secure and verifiable identities in cross-chain transactions. DIDs provide a standard for creating globally unique identifiers that are not tied to any centralized authority. Chain keys, discussed in the previous chapter, serve as cryptographic identities for participants in blockchain networks.

In the architecture of blockchain bridges, DIDs and chain keys contribute to the security and authenticity of cross-chain interactions. They enable participants to be uniquely identified across different blockchains, fostering a trustless environment.

Types of Blockchain Bridge Architectures

The architecture of blockchain bridges is not one-size-fits-all; rather, it adapts to the specific requirements and characteristics of the connected blockchains. Several types of bridge architectures have emerged, each with its own set of advantages and considerations.

1. Pegged Sidechains

Pegged sidechains are a type of bridge architecture where a sidechain is pegged to the main blockchain. The sidechain operates with its consensus mechanism, allowing for faster transaction confirmation times and scalability. Assets are pegged to the main chain by locking them on the main chain while equivalent assets are minted on the sidechain.

This architecture is well-suited for scenarios where the need for faster transactions on a sidechain is balanced with the requirement for security and trustlessness provided by the main chain.

2. Wrapped Tokens

Wrapped tokens involve the creation of a token on one blockchain that represents the value of an asset on another blockchain. For instance, a wrapped Bitcoin (WBTC) on the Ethereum blockchain represents the value of Bitcoin. The wrapped token is backed by the equivalent amount of the underlying asset held in custody.

The architecture relies on trusted custodians to manage the conversion of assets between blockchains. While this introduces a level of centralization, it provides a straightforward and widely adopted solution for representing assets from one blockchain on another.

3. Multi-Signature Wallets

In some bridge architectures, multi-signature wallets are employed to facilitate cross-chain transactions. Multi-signature wallets require multiple private keys to authorize a transaction, distributing trust among different parties.

This architecture enhances security by reducing the risk associated with a single point of failure. Validators or key holders must collectively sign off on transactions, providing a decentralized approach to cross-chain interactions.

4. Cross-Chain Communication Protocols

Cross-chain communication protocols are an essential component of bridge architectures, facilitating the exchange of messages and information between blockchains. These protocols define the rules and standards for how different blockchains communicate and verify transactions.

Interledger Protocol (ILP) and the Polkadot relay chain are examples of cross-chain communication protocols. They enable the seamless transfer of assets and information between interconnected blockchains, forming a foundational layer of the bridge architecture.

Challenges in Bridge Architecture

While the architecture of blockchain bridges offers innovative solutions for cross-chain communication, it is not without its challenges. Recognizing and addressing these challenges is crucial for the continued development and adoption of effective bridge solutions.

1. Security Concerns

Security is a paramount concern in bridge architecture. The reliance on oracles, smart contracts, and validators introduces potential vulnerabilities that malicious actors may exploit. Ensuring the security of the entire bridge network, including the underlying blockchains, is an ongoing challenge that requires robust cryptographic measures and continuous monitoring.

2. Consensus Divergence

Different blockchains may employ diverse consensus mechanisms, introducing challenges in achieving consensus between them. Consensus divergence can lead to discrepancies in transaction finality and validation, impacting the overall security and reliability of the bridge.

Bridges must adapt to handle consensus divergence, potentially requiring complex mechanisms to reconcile differences and ensure a consistent view of cross-chain transactions.

3. Scalability

Scalability remains a persistent challenge in blockchain technology, and bridges are no exception. The architecture must be capable of handling a growing number of interconnected blockchains and an increasing volume of cross-chain transactions.

Efforts to enhance scalability may involve optimizations in the underlying consensus mechanisms, improvements in the efficiency of cross-chain communication protocols, and the development of innovative solutions to accommodate the diverse scalability needs of different blockchains.

4. Regulatory Compliance

The decentralized and borderless nature of blockchain technology poses challenges in terms of regulatory compliance. Bridging assets and information between blockchains may encounter regulatory hurdles related to cross-border transactions, asset transfers, and compliance with data protection laws.

Addressing regulatory challenges requires collaboration between the blockchain industry and regulatory bodies to establish clear frameworks that balance innovation with compliance.

5. Usability and Accessibility

The usability and accessibility of blockchain bridges are critical factors for widespread adoption. Users, including both developers and end-users, should be able to interact with bridges seamlessly. Complicated user interfaces, unclear instructions, and challenging key management processes can hinder the usability of bridge architectures.

Improving the user experience involves designing intuitive interfaces, providing comprehensive documentation, and implementing user-friendly key management solutions. Usability considerations are essential for bridging the gap between blockchain technology and mainstream users.

Future Directions in Bridge Architecture

The architecture of blockchain bridges is poised for continued evolution, driven by advancements in technology and the ever-expanding landscape of blockchain networks. Several directions and trends are likely to shape the future of bridge architecture.

1. Interoperability Standards

The development of interoperability standards is a crucial aspect of future bridge architectures. Standardized protocols for cross-chain communication, smart contract execution, and token locking mechanisms will enhance the interoperability of bridges across diverse blockchains.

Interoperability standards contribute to a more cohesive and collaborative blockchain ecosystem, fostering the seamless exchange of assets and information between different networks.

2. Cross-Chain Communication Improvements

Advancements in cross-chain communication protocols will play a pivotal role in improving the efficiency and reliability of bridges. Innovations such as cross-chain notarization, atomic swaps, and improved message-passing protocols will contribute to faster transaction confirmation times and enhanced security.

The future of bridge architecture involves refining and optimizing communication methods to accommodate the diverse characteristics of interconnected blockchains.

3. Decentralized Oracles and Data Feeds

The reliance on oracles for data feeds introduces a centralization risk. Future bridge architectures may explore decentralized oracle networks that enhance the security and decentralization of data oracles.

Decentralized oracles can contribute to a more trustless and resilient bridge architecture, reducing the reliance on single points of failure in data feeds and information relay.

4. Integration with Layer 2 Solutions

As blockchain networks increasingly explore Layer 2 solutions for scalability, future bridge architectures may integrate with these solutions to leverage their benefits. Layer 2 solutions, such as state channels and sidechains, offer faster transaction confirmation times and reduced fees, enhancing the overall efficiency of cross-chain interactions.

Integrating with Layer 2 solutions can contribute to addressing scalability challenges and providing users with a more seamless and cost-effective experience.

5. Cross-Industry Collaboration

The future of bridge architecture extends beyond the blockchain space. Collaboration with traditional industries, including finance, supply chain, healthcare, and more, will drive the development of specialized bridges that cater to specific use cases.

Cross-industry collaboration may lead to the creation of industry-specific bridge architectures that unlock new opportunities for interoperability and value transfer between blockchain and traditional systems.

6. Enhanced Privacy Features

Privacy considerations will continue to influence the architecture of blockchain bridges. Future advancements may involve the integration of advanced privacy-preserving technologies, such as zero-knowledge proofs, to enhance the confidentiality of cross-chain transactions.

Providing users with the ability to transact across blockchains with increased privacy will contribute to the broader adoption of bridge architectures.

7. Research in Quantum-Resistant Bridges

As the threat of quantum computing advances, future bridge architectures may incorporate quantum-resistant cryptographic techniques to safeguard against potential threats. Research initiatives focused on developing bridges with quantum-resistant features will become increasingly relevant to ensure the long-term security of cross-chain transactions.

Conclusion

The architecture of blockchain bridges stands at the forefront of innovation, enabling the decentralized future of interconnected blockchain networks. By understanding the key components, types, challenges, and future directions in bridge architecture, we gain insight into the complexity and transformative potential of these critical components.

As we progress through subsequent chapters, we will delve into a comparative analysis of interoperability approaches, make a compelling case for trustless interoperability, showcase real-world applications, and envision the future landscape of a unified blockchain ecosystem. The exploration of bridge architecture underscores the dynamic nature of blockchain technology, where collaborative solutions bridge the gaps between isolated networks, fostering a more interconnected and interoperable blockchain ecosystem.

The Role of Oracles and Relayers

In the intricate landscape of blockchain bridges, the seamless exchange of information and assets between disparate blockchain networks relies heavily on two key components: oracles and relayers. These entities act as crucial intermediaries, facilitating cross-chain communication and ensuring the accuracy and trustworthiness of data between interconnected blockchains. This chapter delves into the intricate role of oracles and relayers in the context of blockchain bridges, exploring their functions, challenges, and the evolving landscape that surrounds their integration into decentralized ecosystems.

Oracles: Bridging the Information Gap

Introduction to Oracles

In the decentralized realm of blockchain, oracles play a pivotal role in connecting on-chain smart contracts with real-world data. They act as bridges between the deterministic, trustless environment of blockchains and the inherently non-deterministic, data-rich external world. Oracles enable blockchain-based applications to interact with off-chain data, opening the door to a wide array of use cases, from decentralized finance (DeFi) to supply chain management.

The Functions of Oracles

1. Data Retrieval: At its core, an oracle is responsible for fetching data from external sources, which could include APIs, web services, IoT devices, or any off-chain databases. The accuracy and reliability of this data retrieval process are crucial, as the integrity of smart contracts and decentralized

applications (DApps) relies on the accuracy of the information received.

2. Data Verification: Once the data is retrieved, oracles often play a role in verifying its authenticity. This is especially important in scenarios where the integrity of the data source may be compromised. Various cryptographic techniques, such as zero-knowledge proofs, may be employed to ensure that the data provided to the blockchain is legitimate and has not been tampered with.

3. Data Formatting: The formatting of data is another critical aspect of the oracle's role. Smart contracts typically require data in a specific format, and oracles ensure that the data obtained from external sources is transformed into a format compatible with the blockchain's requirements. This process involves converting real-world data into a format that smart contracts can interpret and use for execution.

4. Data Transmission: Oracles transmit the verified and formatted data onto the blockchain, making it accessible to smart contracts. This transmission is often achieved through the execution of specific transactions on the blockchain, with the data payload containing the relevant information obtained from external sources.

Types of Oracles

1. Centralized Oracles: In a centralized oracle model, a single entity or a group of entities serves as the intermediary between the blockchain and external data sources. While this model is straightforward, it introduces a single point of failure and potential vulnerabilities, as the entire system relies on the trustworthiness of the central oracle.

2. Decentralized Oracles: Decentralized oracles distribute the responsibility across a network of nodes or participants. These nodes collectively contribute to the data retrieval, verification, and transmission processes. Decentralized oracles aim to enhance security and reliability by eliminating the reliance on a single point of control.

3. Consensus-Based Oracles: Consensus-based oracles leverage the collective decision-making power of a group of nodes to determine the accuracy of external data. Nodes within the oracle network come to a consensus on the validity of the data before it is transmitted to the blockchain. This model enhances the trustlessness of the oracle system.

Challenges in Oracle Design

1. Security Risks: Centralized oracles pose security risks, as compromising a single entity could lead to the injection of inaccurate data into the blockchain. Decentralized and consensus-based oracles aim to mitigate these risks, but they are not immune to potential attacks or collusion among participants.

2. Data Source Reliability: The reliability of external data sources is a perpetual challenge for oracles. Malicious actors could manipulate or provide false information to these sources, leading to inaccurate data being fed into smart contracts. Oracles must implement mechanisms to verify and cross-reference information from multiple sources to ensure its accuracy.

3. Oracle Network Consistency: In decentralized and consensus-based oracle networks, achieving consensus on the accuracy of data can be challenging. Nodes may have

different views on the reliability of specific data sources, leading to delays or disagreements in the oracle network. Developing effective consensus mechanisms is crucial for the consistent functioning of decentralized oracles.

4. Data Privacy: Oracles often handle sensitive information obtained from external sources. Ensuring the privacy of this data during the retrieval, verification, and transmission processes is essential. Encryption and privacy-preserving technologies must be integrated into the oracle design to protect the confidentiality of data.

Relayers: Facilitating Cross-Chain Transactions

Introduction to Relayers

Relayers serve as the backbone of blockchain bridges, facilitating the transfer of assets and information between different blockchains. Their role involves receiving, verifying, and transmitting transactions across chains, ensuring that the state of interconnected blockchains remains synchronized. Relayers play a crucial part in achieving the interoperability that bridges aim to provide.

The Functions of Relayers

1. Transaction Reception: Relayers receive transaction requests from users or smart contracts on one blockchain, signaling the intent to transfer assets or information to another blockchain. These transactions are often initiated by users who want to move assets from one blockchain to another for various reasons, such as taking advantage of specific features or participating in decentralized applications on another chain.

2. Verification of Transactions: Once a relayer receives a transaction request, it verifies its legitimacy and ensures that it adheres to the predefined conditions set by the bridge's smart contracts. Verification includes checking the availability of assets for transfer, confirming the validity of the transaction on the source blockchain, and ensuring that the user has the necessary permissions.

3. Interacting with Smart Contracts: Relayers interact with smart contracts on both the source and destination blockchains. Smart contracts govern the conditions under which assets can be locked on the source blockchain and released on the destination blockchain. Relayers execute these smart contracts to initiate and finalize cross-chain transactions, ensuring that the conditions are met and that the transfer is trustless and secure.

4. Cross-Chain Communication: Relayers play a pivotal role in cross-chain communication. They transmit relevant information, such as the transaction details and user signatures, from the source blockchain to the destination blockchain. This communication is essential for coordinating the movement of assets between blockchains in a secure and verifiable manner.

Types of Relayers

1. Centralized Relayers: In a centralized relayer model, a central entity or a consortium of entities manages the relay process. This entity is responsible for coordinating cross-chain transactions, verifying their legitimacy, and executing the necessary steps on both blockchains. While this model may offer simplicity, it introduces a central point of control.

2. Decentralized Relayers: Decentralized relayers distribute the responsibilities across a network of nodes or participants. These nodes collectively contribute to the relay process, making decisions based on a consensus mechanism. Decentralized relayers aim to enhance the security and trustlessness of cross-chain transactions by eliminating a single point of failure.

3. Incentivized Relayers: Incentivized relayers introduce economic incentives to encourage participants to perform the relay function. Participants are rewarded with tokens or other incentives for successfully executing cross-chain transactions. This model aligns with the principles of decentralized finance (DeFi) and aims to attract a network of relayers through economic rewards.

Challenges in Relayer Design

1. Centralization Concerns: Centralized relayers pose a risk of centralization, as a single entity or a consortium controls the relay process. This introduces a vulnerability where the central relayer could potentially manipulate transactions or act against the interests of users. Decentralized and incentivized relayers aim to address these concerns by distributing control and introducing economic incentives.

2. Latency and Throughput: The efficiency of cross-chain transactions relies on the speed at which relayers can process and verify transactions. Latency and throughput challenges may arise, especially in high-traffic scenarios. Optimizing the relay process and exploring scalability

solutions, such as layer 2 technologies, can address these challenges and enhance the overall performance of relayers.

3. Interoperability Standards: Different blockchains may have diverse smart contract languages, consensus mechanisms, and data structures. Achieving interoperability requires relayers to adapt to these differences and facilitate seamless communication. The development and adoption of interoperability standards play a crucial role in ensuring that relayers can effectively relay transactions between blockchains with varying characteristics.

4. Consensus Divergence: Similar to oracles, relayers may encounter challenges related to consensus divergence between blockchains. Different blockchains may have distinct consensus mechanisms and finality models, impacting the synchronization of state across interconnected networks. Developing mechanisms to handle consensus divergence is essential for the reliable functioning of relayers.

Synergy Between Oracles and Relayers

Coordinated Cross-Chain Transactions

The synergy between oracles and relayers is evident in the execution of coordinated cross-chain transactions. Oracles provide the necessary information, such as the state of assets on the source blockchain, to relayers. This information is crucial for relayers to verify and initiate the cross-chain transaction.

Oracles ensure that the data provided to relayers is accurate, reliable, and reflects the current state of the blockchain. Relayers, in turn, leverage this information to execute transactions that adhere to the predefined conditions set by smart contracts on both the source and destination blockchains.

Verifiable and Trustless Transactions

The collaboration between oracles and relayers contributes to the verifiability and trustlessness of cross-chain transactions. Oracles supply the necessary external data, and relayers use this data to execute transactions without the need for trust in centralized entities. Smart contracts governing the relay process ensure that the conditions are met before assets are transferred, providing users with a trustless and secure experience.

Challenges in Synergy

While oracles and relayers work in tandem to enable cross-chain transactions, challenges in their synergy exist:

1. Communication Overhead: Coordinating between oracles and relayers may introduce communication overhead. Ensuring timely and efficient communication between these entities is crucial for the seamless execution of cross-chain transactions.

2. Data Consistency: Maintaining data consistency between oracles and relayers is a challenge, especially in decentralized ecosystems. Discrepancies in data interpretation or delays in data transmission could impact the reliability of cross-chain transactions.

3. Economic Incentives: Aligning economic incentives between oracles and relayers, especially in decentralized and incentivized models, requires careful consideration. Ensuring that both entities are motivated to contribute to the

smooth operation of cross-chain transactions is essential for the sustainability of the ecosystem.

Future Directions in Oracle and Relayer Integration

Enhanced Oracle Capabilities

1. Decentralized Oracle Networks: The evolution of oracles involves a shift toward decentralized oracle networks. These networks distribute the responsibilities of data retrieval, verification, and formatting across a decentralized group of nodes. This approach enhances the security and trustlessness of oracles by eliminating central points of control.

2. Cross-Chain Oracles: Future developments may see the emergence of oracles specifically designed for cross-chain scenarios. These oracles would specialize in providing data relevant to interconnected blockchains, ensuring that the information is suitable for relay and trustless execution of cross-chain transactions.

3. Zero-Knowledge Proofs for Oracles: The integration of advanced cryptographic techniques, such as zero-knowledge proofs, could enhance the privacy and verifiability of data provided by oracles. Zero-knowledge proofs allow oracles to prove the authenticity of data without revealing the actual content, contributing to a more privacy-preserving oracle model.

Evolution of Relayer Architectures

1. Layer 2 Integration: Relayer architectures may integrate with layer 2 solutions to address scalability challenges. Layer 2 solutions, such as state channels or sidechains, offer faster transaction confirmation times and

reduced fees, enhancing the efficiency of cross-chain transactions facilitated by relayers.

2. Enhanced Security Measures: Relayers will likely incorporate enhanced security measures to mitigate risks associated with potential attacks or collusion. Techniques such as multi-signature wallets, threshold cryptography, and hardware-based security modules may be integrated to fortify the security of cross-chain transactions.

3. Interoperability Standards for Relayers: The development and adoption of interoperability standards specific to relayers will contribute to a more seamless and standardized cross-chain communication process. These standards would define common protocols and interfaces that relayers can adhere to, ensuring compatibility across diverse blockchain networks.

Conclusion

The collaboration between oracles and relayers represents a crucial aspect of blockchain bridges, enabling the trustless and secure exchange of assets and information between interconnected blockchains. Oracles bridge the gap between on-chain smart contracts and off-chain data sources, providing the information necessary for relayers to initiate and execute cross-chain transactions.

As we delve into subsequent chapters, exploring a comparative analysis of interoperability approaches, making a compelling case for trustless interoperability, showcasing real-world applications, and envisioning the future landscape of a unified blockchain ecosystem, the roles of oracles and relayers will remain central to the overarching theme of seamless communication and collaboration in the decentralized realm. The continued evolution of these entities promises to unlock new dimensions of trustlessness, privacy, and efficiency in the cross-chain landscape, shaping the future of blockchain interoperability.

The Pitfalls of Bridge-Based Interoperability

In the pursuit of achieving seamless communication and collaboration between disparate blockchain networks, bridge-based interoperability has emerged as a promising solution. While bridges play a crucial role in connecting blockchains and enabling the exchange of assets and information, it is essential to recognize and navigate the potential pitfalls associated with this approach. This chapter delves into the challenges and pitfalls of bridge-based interoperability, exploring issues related to security, consensus divergence, scalability, regulatory compliance, and the broader implications for the decentralized ecosystem.

Security Concerns in Bridge-Based Interoperability

Introduction to Security Challenges

Security is a paramount concern in the realm of blockchain technology, and bridge-based interoperability introduces a set of unique challenges. As bridges facilitate the transfer of assets and data between blockchains, they become potential targets for malicious actors seeking to exploit vulnerabilities in the system. Understanding the security pitfalls is crucial for building robust bridge architectures.

Centralized Points of Failure

One of the primary security pitfalls in bridge-based interoperability is the presence of centralized points of failure. Some bridge architectures may rely on central entities or consortiums to manage key functions such as transaction verification, asset custody, or data relay. In such centralized models, if the central point is compromised, the entire bridge becomes vulnerable to attacks.

Oracle Vulnerabilities

Bridges often depend on oracles to provide external data to the connected blockchains. If oracles are not adequately secured, they become potential points of vulnerability. Malicious actors could manipulate or compromise oracles, leading to inaccurate information being relayed to smart contracts and, consequently, impacting the integrity of cross-chain transactions.

Smart Contract Exploits

Smart contracts governing the operation of bridges are susceptible to exploits and vulnerabilities. If a flaw exists in the code of these smart contracts, it could be exploited to manipulate transactions, compromise assets, or even lead to the loss of funds. Ensuring thorough auditing and testing of smart contract code is crucial to mitigate this security risk.

Data Manipulation Attacks

As data is transmitted between blockchains via bridges, there is a risk of data manipulation attacks. Malicious actors may attempt to alter the information being relayed, leading to discrepancies in the state of interconnected blockchains. Implementing cryptographic techniques, such as digital signatures and hash functions, can help mitigate the risk of data manipulation attacks.

Consensus Divergence and Double-Spending

Consensus divergence poses a significant security challenge in bridge-based interoperability. Different blockchains may have distinct consensus mechanisms and finality models, leading to potential conflicts in the confirmation of cross-chain transactions. Consensus divergence could result in double-spending, where the same assets are spent on multiple blockchains simultaneously.

Consensus Divergence in Bridge-Based Interoperability

Understanding Consensus Divergence

Consensus divergence refers to the situation where different blockchains connected by a bridge may reach conflicting decisions on the validity of a particular transaction. This can occur due to variations in consensus mechanisms, block finality, and the time required to confirm transactions.

Impact on Transaction Finality

Transaction finality is a critical aspect of secure and reliable blockchain operations. In bridge-based interoperability, the consensus divergence may lead to differences in the finality of transactions between interconnected blockchains. A transaction confirmed on one blockchain may be perceived as unconfirmed or conflicting on another, introducing uncertainty and potential vulnerabilities.

Risk of Double-Spending

Consensus divergence introduces the risk of double-spending, a scenario where the same assets are spent on different blockchains simultaneously. This risk undermines the fundamental principle of blockchain, where transactions are intended to be irreversible once confirmed. Addressing the challenge of consensus divergence is essential to prevent double-spending vulnerabilities.

Solutions and Mitigations

1. Cross-Chain Atomic Swaps: Cross-chain atomic swaps are cryptographic techniques that enable the trustless exchange of assets between different blockchains without the need for an intermediary. By using smart contracts with specific conditions, atomic swaps ensure that either the entire transaction is executed or none of it, mitigating the risk of double-spending.

2. Interledger Protocols: Interledger protocols, such as the Interledger Protocol (ILP), provide a framework for secure and interoperable transactions between different payment networks. These protocols facilitate atomic transactions and address consensus divergence challenges by ensuring that the transaction is either fully executed or fully rolled back.

3. Common Consensus Standards: Establishing common consensus standards across interconnected blockchains can help mitigate the risk of consensus divergence. Consistency in consensus mechanisms or the adoption of interoperability standards can contribute to a more synchronized and secure cross-chain transaction environment.

Scalability Challenges in Bridge-Based Interoperability

Scalability as a Crucial Consideration

The scalability of blockchain networks is a persistent challenge, and bridge-based interoperability introduces additional considerations for handling an increased volume of cross-chain transactions. Scalability challenges can impact the efficiency and responsiveness of bridges, limiting their ability to meet the growing demands of interconnected blockchain ecosystems.

Increased Transaction Throughput

As the adoption of blockchain technology grows, the demand for cross-chain transactions is expected to increase significantly. Bridge-based interoperability must address the challenge of accommodating a higher transaction throughput to ensure that assets can be efficiently transferred between blockchains without delays.

Potential Bottlenecks

Certain bridge architectures may introduce potential bottlenecks in the processing of cross-chain transactions. Centralized components or limited throughput capacity can hinder the scalability of bridges, leading to congestion and delayed confirmations. Identifying and mitigating these bottlenecks is crucial for maintaining the efficiency of bridge-based interoperability.

Integration with Layer 2 Solutions

Integrating bridges with Layer 2 solutions can enhance scalability by offloading some transaction processing to secondary layers. Layer 2 solutions, such as state channels or sidechains, offer faster transaction confirmation times and reduced fees, alleviating the strain on the primary blockchain and improving the overall scalability of cross-chain transactions.

Research and Development in Scalability Solutions

Ongoing research and development efforts focus on addressing scalability challenges in blockchain networks. Innovations such as sharding, off-chain scaling solutions, and consensus algorithm optimizations contribute to the broader scalability of interconnected blockchains and, consequently, bridge-based interoperability.

Regulatory Compliance and Legal Implications

Navigating Regulatory Complexity

The decentralized and cross-border nature of blockchain technology introduces regulatory challenges and legal implications for bridge-based interoperability. Navigating the complex landscape of regulations is essential to ensure compliance and avoid legal risks that could impact the operation of bridges and the broader decentralized ecosystem.

Cross-Border Transactions and Jurisdictional Challenges

Interconnected blockchains enable cross-border transactions, raising jurisdictional challenges for regulatory compliance. Different jurisdictions may have varying regulations related to financial transactions, data privacy, and securities, making it challenging to ensure universal compliance for bridge-based interoperability.

Anti-Money Laundering (AML) and Know Your Customer (KYC) Compliance

Regulatory frameworks often require financial institutions to adhere to Anti-Money Laundering (AML) and Know Your Customer (KYC) regulations. Ensuring compliance with these regulations becomes challenging in decentralized environments where users interact with blockchain networks pseudonymously. Addressing AML and KYC requirements while preserving user privacy is a delicate balance.

Smart Contract Legality and Enforceability

The legality and enforceability of smart contracts, which govern the operation of bridges, may vary across jurisdictions. Some legal systems may not explicitly recognize or enforce smart contracts, leading to uncertainties regarding the legal status of transactions conducted through bridge-based interoperability. Engaging with legal experts to navigate jurisdiction-specific legal considerations is crucial.

Cross-Chain Asset Compliance

Bridges facilitate the transfer of assets between blockchains, and these assets may have different regulatory classifications depending on the jurisdictions involved. Ensuring compliance with regulatory frameworks governing the transfer of specific asset types, such as securities or digital assets, is essential to prevent legal challenges.

Potential Solutions and Best Practices

1. Engaging with Regulatory Authorities: Proactively engaging with regulatory authorities and seeking clarity on regulatory requirements can help bridge operators navigate legal complexities. Collaborative efforts between the blockchain industry and regulators contribute to the development of clear frameworks that balance innovation with compliance.

2. Privacy-Preserving Solutions: Implementing privacy-preserving solutions, such as zero-knowledge proofs

or privacy-focused sidechains, can address AML and KYC concerns while maintaining user privacy. These solutions allow for the verification of compliance without revealing sensitive user information.

3. Legal Audits and Compliance Checks: Conducting legal audits and compliance checks, including smart contract audits, can help bridge operators identify and address potential legal risks. Working with legal experts to ensure that smart contracts comply with relevant laws and regulations is a proactive measure to mitigate legal challenges.

4. Asset Tokenization Standards: Establishing and adhering to asset tokenization standards can contribute to regulatory compliance. These standards define the characteristics and regulatory considerations associated with different types of tokenized assets, providing clarity for bridge operators and users alike.

Usability and Accessibility Challenges

User Experience and Adoption Considerations

Usability and accessibility are critical factors for the widespread adoption of bridge-based interoperability. The user experience plays a pivotal role in ensuring that developers and end-users can seamlessly interact with bridges, facilitating the movement of assets and information across blockchains. Addressing usability challenges is essential for realizing the full potential of bridge-based interoperability.

Complex User Interfaces

The complexity of user interfaces for interacting with bridges can present a significant usability challenge. Developers and users may find it challenging to navigate intricate processes related to asset locking, transaction verification, and cross-chain interactions. Simplifying user interfaces and providing comprehensive documentation can enhance the usability of bridge architectures.

Key Management Complexity

Secure key management is integral to the usability and security of bridge-based interoperability. Users need to manage private keys securely to authorize transactions and interact with smart contracts. The complexity of key management processes, including key generation, storage, and recovery, can impact the overall user experience. Introducing user-friendly key management solutions is crucial for broader accessibility.

Educational Barriers

Understanding the intricacies of bridge-based interoperability may pose educational barriers for both developers and end-users. Bridging the gap between technical concepts and user-friendly explanations is essential for fostering a user base that is knowledgeable and comfortable with utilizing bridges for cross-chain transactions.

Transaction Confirmation Delays

The confirmation time for cross-chain transactions is a usability factor that directly impacts the user experience. Lengthy confirmation times can lead to frustration among users, affecting their confidence in the reliability and efficiency of bridge-based interoperability. Optimizing transaction confirmation processes and exploring solutions for faster confirmations contribute to a more user-friendly experience.

Best Practices for Improving Usability

1. Intuitive User Interfaces: Designing intuitive and user-friendly interfaces is paramount for enhancing usability. Clear and straightforward interfaces that guide users through the process of interacting with bridges contribute to a positive user experience.

2. Comprehensive Documentation: Providing comprehensive documentation that explains the functionalities of bridges, step-by-step guides, and troubleshooting resources is essential. Well-documented bridges empower users and developers with the information needed to navigate the complexities of cross-chain interactions.

3. User-Friendly Key Management: Simplifying key management processes and introducing user-friendly solutions, such as hardware wallets or secure key recovery mechanisms, enhances the security and accessibility of bridge-based interoperability.

4. Reduced Confirmation Times: Exploring optimization techniques to reduce transaction confirmation times contributes to a more responsive and efficient user experience. Integration with Layer 2 solutions or enhancements to the underlying consensus mechanisms can address delays in confirmation.

Future Directions in Bridge-Based Interoperability

Continued Evolution and Innovation

The pitfalls discussed in this chapter highlight the challenges that bridge-based interoperability must address to reach its full potential. However, ongoing research, development, and innovation in the blockchain space continue to pave the way for solutions that mitigate these pitfalls and contribute to the continued evolution of bridge architectures.

Decentralized and Trustless Bridge Models

The future of bridge-based interoperability involves a shift towards more decentralized and trustless models. Efforts to eliminate centralized points of failure, enhance security through cryptographic techniques, and distribute responsibilities across decentralized networks aim to create bridge architectures that align with the principles of blockchain technology.

Scalability Solutions and Layer 2 Integration

Scalability challenges are expected to be addressed through the integration of scalable solutions and Layer 2 technologies. Research initiatives focusing on sharding, off-chain scaling, and optimizations in consensus algorithms will contribute to the scalability of interconnected blockchains and, consequently, bridge-based interoperability.

Regulatory Frameworks and Standards

As the blockchain industry matures, collaboration between the industry and regulatory bodies will play a crucial role in developing clear frameworks and standards for bridge-based interoperability. Establishing regulatory compliance standards, privacy-preserving solutions, and interoperability frameworks will contribute to a more secure and legally compliant cross-chain ecosystem.

Enhanced Usability and User Education

Improving usability and user education will be central to driving adoption of bridge-based interoperability. Future developments will likely prioritize the design of intuitive interfaces, user-friendly key management solutions, and educational resources that empower users to confidently interact with bridges and participate in cross-chain transactions.

Interoperability Research and Collaboration

Interoperability research will continue to explore novel approaches and collaborative solutions. Cross-industry collaboration, academic research, and open-source development efforts will contribute to the exploration of innovative interoperability models, addressing the pitfalls discussed in this chapter and shaping the future of decentralized communication between blockchains.

Conclusion

Bridge-based interoperability holds the promise of creating a unified and interconnected blockchain ecosystem. However, navigating the pitfalls associated with security concerns, consensus divergence, scalability challenges, regulatory compliance, and usability issues is crucial for the successful implementation of bridges.

As blockchain technology continues to evolve, the lessons learned from addressing these pitfalls will inform the development of more robust, secure, and user-friendly bridge architectures. The collaborative efforts of researchers, developers, regulators, and the broader blockchain community will play a pivotal role in shaping the future of bridge-based interoperability, fostering a decentralized landscape where assets and information can seamlessly flow between interconnected blockchains.

Evaluating the Security and Reliability of Bridges

Bridges play a pivotal role in connecting disparate blockchain networks, facilitating the exchange of assets and information in a decentralized ecosystem. As the demand for interoperability grows, evaluating the security and reliability of bridges becomes paramount. This chapter explores the intricate aspects of bridge security, the challenges they face, and the measures taken to ensure the reliability of cross-chain interactions.

Security Considerations in Bridge Architecture

Introduction to Bridge Security

Security is a cornerstone of blockchain technology, and bridges, acting as conduits between different blockchains, must adhere to robust security standards. Evaluating the security of bridge architecture involves examining various components, from smart contracts and oracles to consensus mechanisms and data transmission protocols.

Smart Contract Security

Smart contracts govern the operations of bridges, defining the rules for asset transfers and ensuring the trustless execution of cross-chain transactions. However, vulnerabilities in smart contract code can be exploited, leading to potential security breaches. Regular audits and code reviews by security experts are essential to identify and address these vulnerabilities, enhancing the overall security of bridge-based interoperability.

Decentralization and Single Points of Failure

The degree of decentralization in bridge architecture is a critical factor in assessing security. Centralized points of failure introduce vulnerabilities, as compromising a single entity could jeopardize the entire bridge network. Decentralized bridge models distribute responsibilities across a network of nodes, reducing the risk of a single point of failure and enhancing the security of cross-chain transactions.

Oracle Security

Oracles play a crucial role in providing external data to smart contracts, influencing the accuracy and reliability of cross-chain transactions. Securing oracles is vital to prevent data manipulation attacks and ensure the integrity of the information relayed to the blockchain. Implementing cryptographic techniques, multi-sourcing data, and leveraging decentralized oracle networks contribute to the overall security of bridges.

Consensus Mechanisms and Finality

The choice of consensus mechanisms in bridge architecture impacts security and transaction finality. Consensus divergence, where interconnected blockchains reach conflicting decisions, introduces security risks such as double-spending. Ensuring consistency in consensus mechanisms or employing mechanisms that address divergence is essential for secure and reliable cross-chain transactions.

Data Transmission Security

The secure transmission of data between blockchains is a crucial aspect of bridge security. Encryption, digital signatures, and secure communication protocols safeguard data during transmission, mitigating the risk of interception or manipulation. Implementing robust security measures at the data transmission layer contributes to the overall security of bridges.

Challenges and Vulnerabilities in Bridge Security

Centralization Risks

Centralization poses inherent risks to bridge security. In scenarios where a single entity or consortium manages key functions of the bridge, such as transaction verification or data relay, the concentration of control becomes a potential point of vulnerability. Malicious actors targeting centralized points of failure could compromise the security of the entire bridge network.

Oracle Exploits

Oracles, while essential for providing external data, introduce a vector for potential exploits. Malicious actors may attempt to compromise or manipulate oracles to feed inaccurate information to smart contracts. This manipulation can lead to undesirable outcomes, such as erroneous asset transfers or disruptions in cross-chain transactions.

Smart Contract Vulnerabilities

Smart contracts governing bridge operations are susceptible to vulnerabilities and exploits. Flaws in smart contract code could be exploited to manipulate transaction outcomes, compromise asset custody, or lead to unauthorized access. Rigorous smart contract audits, code reviews, and adherence to best practices are crucial for mitigating these vulnerabilities.

Consensus Divergence and Double-Spending

Consensus divergence between interconnected blockchains introduces the risk of double-spending. Conflicting decisions on the validity of a transaction may lead to discrepancies in the state of assets on different blockchains. Addressing consensus divergence is essential to prevent the duplication of assets and maintain the integrity of cross-chain transactions.

Data Manipulation Attacks

Bridges are susceptible to data manipulation attacks during the transmission of information between blockchains. Malicious actors may attempt to alter the data being relayed, leading to inconsistencies in the state of interconnected blockchains. Ensuring data integrity through cryptographic measures is crucial for preventing data manipulation attacks.

Security Best Practices in Bridge Development

Decentralized Architecture

Embracing a decentralized architecture is a fundamental best practice for enhancing bridge security. Distributing responsibilities across a network of nodes or validators reduces the risk of central points of failure. Decentralized bridge models align with the principles of blockchain technology, fostering a trustless and secure environment for cross-chain transactions.

Smart Contract Audits

Regular and thorough smart contract audits are critical for identifying and mitigating vulnerabilities in bridge operations. Engaging with reputable auditing firms or security experts to conduct comprehensive audits of smart contract code ensures that potential exploits are discovered and addressed before deployment.

Secure Key Management

Secure key management is integral to user security and the overall reliability of bridge-based interoperability. Implementing robust key management practices, including secure key generation, storage, and recovery mechanisms, minimizes the risk of unauthorized access and ensures the integrity of user assets.

Multi-Sourcing Data for Oracles

To enhance the reliability of oracles, multi-sourcing data from diverse and reputable sources is a recommended best practice. Utilizing decentralized oracle networks or aggregating information from multiple independent oracles reduces the likelihood of inaccurate data being relayed to smart contracts, improving the overall security of bridges.

Consensus Mechanism Consistency

Ensuring consistency in consensus mechanisms across interconnected blockchains is vital for preventing consensus divergence. Compatibility in consensus models reduces the risk of conflicting decisions on transaction validity, mitigating the potential for double-spending and maintaining a synchronized state across blockchains.

Data Encryption and Secure Transmission

Implementing robust encryption methods and secure communication protocols for data transmission enhances the security of bridges. Encrypting data during transmission and employing digital signatures provide layers of protection against interception and manipulation, safeguarding the integrity of cross-chain transactions.

Reliability in Cross-Chain Transactions

Introduction to Reliability in Bridges

Reliability is a key aspect of bridge-based interoperability, ensuring that cross-chain transactions are executed securely and efficiently. Evaluating the reliability of bridges involves assessing factors such as transaction confirmation times, scalability, and the overall responsiveness of the bridge network.

Transaction Confirmation Times

The time taken to confirm cross-chain transactions directly impacts user experience and the efficiency of bridge-based interoperability. Lengthy confirmation times can lead to user frustration and may affect the perceived reliability of bridges. Implementing optimization techniques and exploring solutions for faster confirmations contribute to the reliability of cross-chain transactions.

Scalability Challenges

Scalability is a critical consideration in ensuring the reliability of bridge networks, especially as the volume of cross-chain transactions increases. Potential bottlenecks in transaction processing can hinder scalability, leading to congestion and delays. Integrating bridges with Layer 2 solutions or exploring innovations in consensus algorithms contributes to improved scalability and overall reliability.

User-Friendly Interfaces

The reliability of bridge-based interoperability extends to user interfaces that developers and end-users interact with. Complex user interfaces may hinder the adoption of bridges, as users may find it challenging to navigate intricate processes. Designing intuitive and user-friendly interfaces is essential for enhancing the reliability of bridges and promoting broader accessibility.

Educational Resources and Support

Reliability also encompasses user education and support. Providing comprehensive documentation, tutorials, and support resources empowers users and developers to confidently interact with bridges. Educational initiatives that bridge the gap between technical concepts and user-friendly explanations contribute to the overall reliability of bridge-based interoperability.

Challenges and Solutions in Achieving Reliability

Transaction Confirmation Delays

Transaction confirmation delays pose a significant challenge to the reliability of bridge-based interoperability. Factors such as network congestion, processing bottlenecks, and consensus mechanisms can contribute to delays in confirming cross-chain transactions. Addressing these challenges involves optimizing transaction processing, exploring scalability solutions, and adopting mechanisms for faster confirmations.

Scalability Bottlenecks

Potential bottlenecks in transaction processing represent a challenge to the reliability of bridges. Centralized components or limited throughput capacity can hinder scalability, leading to congestion and delayed confirmations. Identifying and mitigating these bottlenecks through the integration of scalable solutions and optimizations in bridge architecture contribute to improved reliability.

User Interface Complexity

Complex user interfaces can hinder the reliability of bridge-based interoperability. Developers and users may face challenges in navigating intricate processes related to asset locking, transaction verification, and cross-chain interactions. Streamlining user interfaces, providing clear guidance, and offering user-friendly experiences contribute to the reliability of bridges.

Educational Barriers

Educational barriers pose a challenge to the reliability of bridges, especially when users and developers struggle to understand the intricacies of cross-chain interactions. Fostering a knowledgeable user base through comprehensive documentation, tutorials, and educational initiatives is crucial for overcoming educational barriers and enhancing the reliability of bridge-based interoperability.

Future Directions in Bridge Security and Reliability

Continuous Innovation and Research

The landscape of bridge-based interoperability is dynamic, with ongoing innovation and research addressing security and reliability challenges. The future holds promising developments in decentralized bridge models, enhanced security measures, and improved scalability solutions. Collaboration between industry stakeholders, academic researchers, and the broader blockchain community will play a pivotal role in shaping the evolution of bridge security and reliability.

Decentralized Bridge Models

The future of bridge security involves a transition towards more decentralized and trustless models. Efforts to eliminate centralized points of failure, enhance security through cryptographic techniques, and distribute responsibilities across decentralized networks aim to create bridge architectures that align with the principles of blockchain technology.

Advanced Security Measures

Advancements in security measures will contribute to the robustness of bridge-based interoperability. Integration of advanced cryptographic techniques, such as zero-knowledge proofs, homomorphic encryption, and threshold cryptography, will enhance the privacy, integrity, and security of cross-chain transactions. Ongoing research in secure key management and oracle security will also play a crucial role in advancing bridge security.

Scalability Solutions and Layer 2 Integration

Scalability remains a focal point for future developments in bridge reliability. Integration with Layer 2 solutions, innovations in consensus algorithms, and advancements in sharding techniques will address scalability challenges. Research initiatives exploring novel approaches to enhance transaction throughput and reduce confirmation times will contribute to the overall reliability of bridge networks.

User-Centric Designs and Educational Initiatives

Future directions in bridge reliability emphasize user-centric designs and educational initiatives. Improving user interfaces, simplifying key management processes, and providing educational resources will foster a user base that is knowledgeable and comfortable with utilizing bridges for cross-chain transactions. Bridging the gap between technical complexity and user-friendly experiences will be central to achieving widespread adoption and reliability.

Regulatory Compliance and Legal Considerations

The evolving regulatory landscape introduces considerations for the security and reliability of bridges. Future developments will likely involve collaborative efforts between the blockchain industry and regulatory bodies to establish clear frameworks, compliance standards, and legal considerations for bridge-based interoperability. Engaging with regulatory authorities and proactively addressing legal challenges will contribute to the long-term reliability of bridge networks.

Conclusion

Evaluating the security and reliability of bridges is crucial for the successful implementation of cross-chain interoperability. Security considerations encompass various aspects, including smart contract security, decentralization, oracle security, consensus mechanisms, and data transmission security. Addressing challenges such as centralization risks, oracle exploits, smart contract vulnerabilities, consensus divergence, and data manipulation attacks is essential for building robust and secure bridges.

Reliability, on the other hand, extends to factors such as transaction confirmation times, scalability, user-friendly interfaces, and educational resources. Overcoming challenges related to transaction confirmation delays, scalability bottlenecks, user interface complexity, and educational barriers contributes to the overall reliability of bridge-based interoperability.

As the blockchain industry continues to evolve, continuous innovation, research, and collaboration will shape the future of bridge security and reliability. Decentralized bridge models, advanced security measures, scalability solutions, user-centric designs, and regulatory compliance will be key drivers in ensuring the secure and reliable flow of assets and information between interconnected blockchains.

Exploring Future Directions in Bridge Design

The evolution of blockchain technology has been marked by continuous innovation and a quest for enhanced interoperability. As bridges play a pivotal role in connecting disparate blockchains, exploring future directions in bridge design becomes paramount. This chapter delves into the cutting-edge developments and emerging trends that are shaping the future of bridge-based interoperability, with a focus on decentralized models, advanced cryptographic techniques, scalability solutions, and the integration of artificial intelligence.

Decentralized Bridge Models

The future of bridge design is gravitating towards decentralized and trustless models that align with the core principles of blockchain technology. Centralization introduces vulnerabilities, and efforts are underway to eliminate single points of failure in bridge architecture. Decentralized bridge models distribute responsibilities across a network of nodes, reducing the risk of manipulation, censorship, and compromise. This shift towards decentralization fosters a more resilient and secure cross-chain ecosystem.

Eliminating Centralized Points of Failure

One of the primary objectives in future bridge design is the elimination of centralized points of failure. In traditional bridge architectures, certain components may rely on central entities or consortiums to manage key functions, such as transaction verification or data relay. Decentralized models distribute these functions across a network of nodes, ensuring that no single entity has control over critical aspects of the bridge. This not only enhances security but also aligns with the decentralized ethos of blockchain technology.

Decentralized Oracles and Data Sourcing

Oracles play a crucial role in providing external data to smart contracts within bridge-based interoperability. Future bridge designs explore the use of decentralized oracles that source information from diverse and independent data feeds. Decentralized oracles reduce the risk of manipulation or data inaccuracies by aggregating information from multiple, uncorrelated sources. This approach enhances the reliability of external data and minimizes the potential impact of a compromised oracle on cross-chain transactions.

Cryptography and Privacy-Preserving Techniques

The future of bridge design involves advancements in cryptographic techniques, with a focus on enhancing privacy, security, and the trustless nature of cross-chain transactions. Cryptographic primitives such as zero-knowledge proofs, homomorphic encryption, and threshold cryptography are gaining prominence. These techniques allow for the secure transfer of assets and information between blockchains without revealing sensitive data, contributing to the privacy and confidentiality of cross-chain interactions.

Zero-Knowledge Proofs in Bridge Design

Zero-knowledge proofs, particularly zk-SNARKs (Zero-Knowledge Succinct Non-Interactive Arguments of Knowledge), are emerging as powerful tools in the arsenal of cryptographic techniques for bridge design. These proofs enable one party to prove the knowledge of certain information without revealing that information itself. In the context of bridges, zero-knowledge proofs can be employed to verify the validity of transactions without exposing the transaction details, significantly enhancing the privacy and security of cross-chain transactions.

Homomorphic Encryption for Secure Data Transmission

Homomorphic encryption is a cryptographic technique that allows computations to be performed on encrypted data without decrypting it. In bridge design, homomorphic encryption can be applied to secure the transmission of sensitive information between blockchains. This ensures that data remains confidential during transit, reducing the risk of interception or manipulation. Homomorphic encryption contributes to the overall security and integrity of cross-chain transactions.

Threshold Cryptography for Enhanced Security

Threshold cryptography involves distributing cryptographic keys among multiple parties, requiring a threshold number of parties to collaborate to perform cryptographic operations. In the context of bridge design, threshold cryptography enhances security by eliminating the reliance on a single entity for key management. Even if some key shares are compromised, the collaborative effort required to reconstruct the full key adds an additional layer of security to the bridge network.

Scalability Solutions for Cross-Chain Transactions

Scalability remains a critical consideration in the design of future bridges, especially as the demand for cross-chain transactions continues to grow. Several innovative solutions are being explored to address scalability challenges and enhance the efficiency of bridge networks.

Sharding Techniques for Improved Throughput

Sharding involves partitioning the blockchain into smaller, more manageable segments called shards. Each shard operates independently, processing its transactions and smart contracts. In the context of bridges, sharding can improve throughput by allowing multiple cross-chain transactions to occur concurrently across different shards. This approach enhances the scalability of bridge networks, accommodating a higher volume of transactions without compromising security.

Layer 2 Solutions and Off-Chain Scaling

Integrating bridges with Layer 2 solutions is a promising avenue for improving scalability. Layer 2 solutions, such as state channels and sidechains, enable off-chain scaling by processing transactions outside the main blockchain. This reduces congestion on the primary blockchain, resulting in faster confirmation times and lower transaction fees. The integration of Layer 2 solutions contributes to the overall scalability and responsiveness of bridge networks.

Dynamic Block Size Adjustments

Dynamic block size adjustments represent an adaptive approach to scalability. In future bridge designs, the block size can dynamically adjust based on network demand.

During periods of high activity, the block size can increase to accommodate a larger number of transactions, while it can decrease during periods of lower demand. This dynamic adjustment optimizes resource utilization and responsiveness, ensuring that the bridge network can efficiently handle varying transaction volumes.

Interoperability Standards and Cross-Chain Communication Protocols

Interoperability standards and cross-chain communication protocols are pivotal in shaping the future of bridge-based interoperability. Standardizing the way different blockchains communicate and share information fosters a more seamless and efficient cross-chain ecosystem. The development and adoption of interoperability standards enable diverse blockchains to interoperate, paving the way for a unified and interconnected blockchain landscape.

Interledger Protocols for Cross-Chain Transactions

Interledger protocols, such as the Interledger Protocol (ILP), provide a standardized framework for secure and interoperable transactions between different payment networks. In the context of bridge design, Interledger protocols can facilitate cross-chain transactions by defining a common protocol for value transfer. This approach simplifies the process of exchanging assets between blockchains, contributing to a more interoperable and interconnected blockchain ecosystem.

Cross-Chain Atomic Swaps for Trustless Asset Exchange

Cross-chain atomic swaps are cryptographic techniques that enable the trustless exchange of assets between different blockchains without the need for an intermediary. Future bridge designs may incorporate cross-chain atomic swaps to facilitate secure and decentralized asset exchanges. By utilizing smart contracts with specific conditions, atomic swaps ensure that either the entire transaction is executed, or none of it, mitigating the risk of fraud or manipulation.

Integration of Artificial Intelligence in Bridge Security

The integration of artificial intelligence (AI) holds promise in enhancing the security and efficiency of bridge-based interoperability. AI algorithms can be employed for real-time threat detection, anomaly detection, and predictive analysis, bolstering the overall security posture of bridge networks.

Real-Time Threat Detection and Prevention

AI-driven threat detection systems can continuously monitor the bridge network for potential security threats. By analyzing patterns and behaviors in real-time, AI algorithms can identify and respond to malicious activities, mitigating security risks before they escalate. This proactive approach enhances the overall security resilience of bridge-based interoperability.

Anomaly Detection for Abnormal Behavior

AI-powered anomaly detection mechanisms can identify abnormal behavior or deviations from established patterns within the bridge network. Unusual patterns, such as unexpected transaction volumes or atypical data transmissions, can be flagged for further investigation. Anomaly detection contributes to the early detection of potential security breaches and ensures a rapid response to emerging threats.

Predictive Analysis for Anticipating Security Trends

The integration of AI for predictive analysis enables bridge networks to anticipate and adapt to evolving security trends. By analyzing historical data, identifying patterns, and considering external factors, AI algorithms can forecast potential security challenges. This forward-looking approach empowers bridge operators to implement preemptive security measures and stay ahead of emerging threats.

User-Centric Designs and Enhanced Usability

The future of bridge design places a strong emphasis on user-centric designs and enhanced usability. Improving the user experience for both developers and end-users is crucial for driving widespread adoption of bridge-based interoperability.

Intuitive User Interfaces for Seamless Interaction

Designing intuitive and user-friendly interfaces is a key consideration in future bridge designs. Clear and straightforward interfaces guide users through the process of interacting with bridges, making it easier for developers and end-users to participate in cross-chain transactions. Intuitive interfaces contribute to a positive user experience and foster broader accessibility.

Simplified Key Management Processes

Secure key management is integral to the usability and security of bridge-based interoperability. Future designs aim to simplify key management processes, including key generation, storage, and recovery. User-friendly solutions, such as hardware wallets or secure key recovery mechanisms, enhance the security and accessibility of bridge networks, making them more user-friendly.

Comprehensive Educational Resources

Overcoming educational barriers is crucial for the widespread adoption of bridge-based interoperability. Future designs prioritize the development of comprehensive educational resources, including documentation, tutorials, and support materials. Bridging the gap between technical concepts and user-friendly explanations empowers users and developers with the knowledge needed to confidently interact with bridges.

Usability Testing and Continuous Improvement

Usability testing is an ongoing process in future bridge designs to identify areas for improvement in user interfaces and overall user experience. Collecting feedback from developers and end-users allows for continuous refinement of bridge designs, ensuring that usability challenges are addressed, and the overall user experience is optimized.

Regulatory Compliance and Legal Considerations

As the blockchain industry matures, regulatory compliance and legal considerations become integral aspects of bridge design. Future bridges are expected to navigate regulatory frameworks, adhere to compliance standards, and address legal challenges associated with cross-chain transactions.

Engaging with Regulatory Authorities

Proactively engaging with regulatory authorities and seeking clarity on regulatory requirements are essential components of future bridge designs. Collaboration between the blockchain industry and regulators contributes to the development of clear frameworks that balance innovation with compliance. This collaborative approach fosters a regulatory environment that supports the growth of bridge-based interoperability.

Privacy-Preserving Solutions for Regulatory Compliance

Addressing privacy concerns while ensuring regulatory compliance is a challenge in decentralized environments. Future bridge designs may incorporate privacy-preserving solutions, such as zero-knowledge proofs or privacy-focused sidechains. These solutions allow for the verification of compliance without revealing sensitive user information, aligning with regulatory requirements while maintaining user privacy.

Legal Audits and Compliance Checks

Conducting legal audits and compliance checks, including smart contract audits, is a proactive measure in future bridge designs. Ensuring that bridge operations comply with relevant laws and regulations helps bridge operators identify and address potential legal risks. Working with legal experts to navigate jurisdiction-specific legal considerations contributes to regulatory compliance.

Asset Tokenization Standards

Future bridge designs may establish and adhere to asset tokenization standards to facilitate regulatory compliance. These standards define the characteristics and regulatory considerations associated with different types of tokenized assets, providing clarity for bridge operators and users alike. Adhering to these standards contributes to a more transparent and compliant cross-chain ecosystem.

Conclusion

The future of bridge-based interoperability is characterized by a convergence of decentralized models, advanced cryptographic techniques, scalability solutions, and user-centric designs. Decentralized bridge models eliminate centralized points of failure, ensuring a more resilient and secure cross-chain ecosystem. Advanced cryptographic techniques, including zero-knowledge proofs, homomorphic encryption, and threshold cryptography, enhance the privacy, security, and trustlessness of cross-chain transactions.

Scalability solutions, such as sharding, Layer 2 integration, and dynamic block size adjustments, address the growing demand for cross-chain transactions. Interoperability standards and cross-chain communication protocols contribute to a more seamless and efficient cross-chain ecosystem, allowing diverse blockchains to interoperate.

The integration of artificial intelligence in bridge security introduces real-time threat detection, anomaly detection, and predictive analysis, bolstering the overall security resilience of bridge networks. User-centric designs and enhanced usability prioritize intuitive interfaces, simplified key management processes, and comprehensive educational resources, fostering a positive user experience and driving widespread adoption.

Regulatory compliance and legal considerations become integral aspects of future bridge designs, with a focus on engaging with regulatory authorities, implementing privacy-preserving solutions, conducting legal audits, and adhering to asset tokenization standards. The collaborative efforts of industry stakeholders, developers, regulators, and the broader blockchain community will play a pivotal role in shaping the future of bridge-based interoperability, fostering a decentralized landscape where assets and information can seamlessly flow between interconnected blockchains.

Chapter 3: A Comparative Analysis of Interoperability Approaches

Chain Keys vs. Bridges: A Comprehensive Comparison

In the dynamic landscape of blockchain interoperability, two prominent approaches have emerged to address the challenges of connecting disparate blockchain networks: Chain Keys and Bridges. Each approach offers unique solutions and introduces distinct trade-offs. This comprehensive comparison delves into the intricacies of Chain Keys and Bridges, exploring their fundamental concepts, strengths, weaknesses, and real-world applications.

Fundamental Concepts

Chain Keys:

Chain Keys, at their core, are cryptographic keys associated with specific blockchain networks. These keys play a crucial role in enabling trustless communication between blockchains. Chain Keys are utilized to establish a secure connection and verify the authenticity of cross-chain transactions. The essence of Chain Keys lies in their ability to facilitate interoperability without relying on centralized or trusted third parties.

Bridges:

Bridges, on the other hand, serve as intermediary entities that facilitate communication and asset transfer between different blockchains. These can take various forms, including smart contracts, protocols, or dedicated networks. The fundamental concept of bridges revolves around providing a seamless and secure conduit for information and value to flow between otherwise isolated blockchain ecosystems.

Strengths

Chain Keys:

1. Trustless Interaction: Chain Keys offer a trustless model, eliminating the need for reliance on intermediaries or centralized entities. The cryptographic nature of Chain Keys ensures that cross-chain transactions can be securely executed without the need for trust in third parties.

2. Enhanced Security: The security advantages of Chain Keys lie in their cryptographic properties. Through the use of robust encryption algorithms, Chain Keys contribute to the confidentiality and integrity of communication between interconnected blockchains.

3. Decentralization: Chain Keys promote decentralization by allowing blockchain networks to interact directly without intermediaries. This aligns with the core principles of blockchain technology, fostering a distributed and decentralized ecosystem.

4. Privacy Preservation: Chain Keys can be designed to preserve user privacy by employing techniques such as zero-knowledge proofs. This ensures that the details of a transaction can be verified without revealing sensitive information.

Bridges:

1. Versatility: Bridges offer a versatile solution that can be implemented in various forms, including smart contracts, dedicated networks, or specialized protocols. This

adaptability allows bridges to cater to different blockchain ecosystems and use cases.

2. Scalability: Bridges contribute to scalability by facilitating cross-chain transactions outside the main blockchain. This off-chain processing reduces congestion and enhances the overall throughput of the interconnected blockchain networks.

3. Interoperability Standards: Many bridges adhere to interoperability standards and protocols, providing a common framework for different blockchains to communicate. This standardization fosters a more seamless and efficient cross-chain ecosystem.

4. Consensus Flexibility: Depending on the implementation, bridges can offer flexibility in choosing consensus mechanisms. This adaptability allows bridges to connect blockchains with varying consensus models, promoting compatibility.

Weaknesses

Chain Keys:

1. Scalability Challenges: Chain Keys may face scalability challenges as the number of interconnected blockchains increases. Each additional connection requires the management of unique Chain Keys, potentially introducing complexities in key management and communication.

2. Limited Use Cases: The application of Chain Keys may be limited to specific use cases or scenarios where direct, trustless interaction between blockchains is essential. In situations where intermediary entities or additional

functionalities are required, Chain Keys alone may not suffice.

3. Technical Complexity: Implementing and managing Chain Keys may involve technical complexities, particularly for users who are not well-versed in cryptographic concepts. User education and user-friendly interfaces are crucial to overcoming these challenges.

Bridges:

1. Centralization Risks: Depending on the design, some bridges may introduce centralization risks. Centralized components or oracles within the bridge architecture could become potential points of failure, compromising the trustless nature of cross-chain transactions.

2. Security Vulnerabilities: Bridges, especially those relying on smart contracts, are susceptible to security vulnerabilities. Flaws in smart contract code or vulnerabilities in the bridge architecture may be exploited by malicious actors, leading to potential security breaches.

3. Reliance on Trusted Oracles: Certain bridge designs may rely on trusted oracles to relay information between blockchains. This introduces a level of reliance on external entities, and the compromise of trusted oracles could impact the overall security and trustlessness of the bridge.

4. Privacy Concerns: Depending on the implementation, bridges may face challenges in preserving user privacy. The relay of information between blockchains may expose transaction details, raising concerns about data confidentiality.

Real-World Applications

Chain Keys:

1. Cross-Chain Asset Transfers: Chain Keys find practical application in enabling cross-chain asset transfers. Users can securely move assets from one blockchain to another, leveraging the trustless nature of Chain Keys for verification.

2. Decentralized Finance (DeFi): In the realm of decentralized finance, Chain Keys play a crucial role in facilitating trustless interactions between different financial protocols and blockchain ecosystems. This includes scenarios such as decentralized exchanges and lending platforms.

3. Privacy-Preserving Transactions: Chain Keys can be utilized to enhance privacy in transactions, especially when combined with techniques like zero-knowledge proofs. This makes them suitable for applications where preserving user privacy is a priority.

Bridges:

1. Interoperable Token Swaps: Bridges facilitate interoperable token swaps, allowing users to exchange tokens between different blockchains seamlessly. This application is particularly relevant in scenarios where users want to leverage assets from multiple blockchain ecosystems.

2. Cross-Chain Smart Contracts: Bridges enable the execution of cross-chain smart contracts, extending the functionality of decentralized applications (DApps) to interact with multiple blockchains. This is valuable in scenarios where DApps require inputs or triggers from different blockchain sources.

3. Decentralized Identity Management: Some bridge implementations contribute to decentralized identity management, allowing users to interact with applications and services across various blockchain networks using a unified identity.

Conclusion

The comparison between Chain Keys and Bridges highlights the nuanced strengths, weaknesses, and applications of each approach. Chain Keys offer a trustless and decentralized model, particularly suitable for scenarios where direct interaction between blockchains is paramount, and user privacy is a priority. On the other hand, Bridges provide versatility and scalability, catering to diverse use cases and promoting interoperability among different blockchain ecosystems.

The choice between Chain Keys and Bridges depends on the specific requirements of the use case, the desired level of trustlessness, and the need for scalability. In some scenarios, a hybrid approach that combines the strengths of both Chain Keys and Bridges may emerge as a practical solution, offering a balanced compromise between security, versatility, and scalability. As the blockchain industry continues to evolve, the ongoing exploration and refinement of these interoperability approaches will shape the interconnected future of blockchain ecosystems.

Evaluating the Pros and Cons of Chain Keys

In the ever-evolving landscape of blockchain interoperability, Chain Keys have emerged as a novel and promising approach. This section conducts a comprehensive evaluation of the strengths and weaknesses inherent in the utilization of Chain Keys for facilitating trustless communication between different blockchain networks.

Pros of Chain Keys:

1. Trustless Interaction:

Chain Keys fundamentally operate on the principle of trustless interaction. By employing cryptographic keys associated with specific blockchains, Chain Keys enable secure communication without the need for centralized intermediaries or trusted third parties. This trustlessness aligns with the core tenets of blockchain technology, fostering a decentralized and resilient ecosystem.

2. Enhanced Security:

Security is a paramount consideration in blockchain ecosystems, and Chain Keys contribute significantly to enhancing the overall security of cross-chain transactions. The cryptographic nature of Chain Keys ensures the confidentiality and integrity of communication between interconnected blockchains. This robust security framework minimizes the risk of unauthorized access, tampering, or manipulation of data during cross-chain interactions.

3. Decentralization:

Decentralization is a foundational principle in blockchain technology, and Chain Keys reinforce this ethos. By facilitating direct communication between blockchains without relying on centralized entities, Chain Keys contribute to the decentralization of cross-chain transactions. This distributed approach reduces the vulnerability of the system to single points of failure and enhances the overall resilience of the interconnected blockchain network.

4. Privacy Preservation:

Chain Keys offer a pathway to privacy preservation in cross-chain transactions. Through the application of cryptographic techniques, such as zero-knowledge proofs, Chain Keys can be designed to verify the validity of transactions without exposing sensitive information. This privacy-centric feature is particularly advantageous in scenarios where user confidentiality is a priority.

5. Real-World Applications:

Chain Keys find practical applications in various real-world scenarios, showcasing their versatility. One notable application is in facilitating cross-chain asset transfers. Users can securely move assets from one blockchain to another, leveraging the trustless nature of Chain Keys for verification. Additionally, Chain Keys play a crucial role in decentralized finance (DeFi), enabling trustless interactions between different financial protocols and blockchain ecosystems.

Cons of Chain Keys:

1. Scalability Challenges:

While Chain Keys offer a trustless model for cross-chain interactions, they may encounter scalability challenges as the number of interconnected blockchains increases. Each additional connection requires the management of unique

Chain Keys, potentially introducing complexities in key management and communication. This scalability concern needs to be addressed to ensure the seamless expansion of cross-chain interoperability.

2. Limited Use Cases:

The application of Chain Keys may be limited to specific use cases where direct, trustless interaction between blockchains is essential. In situations where intermediary entities or additional functionalities are required, Chain Keys alone may not suffice. This limitation may hinder the broader adoption of Chain Keys in diverse cross-chain scenarios.

3. Technical Complexity:

Implementing and managing Chain Keys may involve technical complexities, particularly for users who are not well-versed in cryptographic concepts. The secure generation, storage, and handling of Chain Keys require a certain level of technical proficiency. Overcoming this challenge involves providing user-friendly interfaces and comprehensive educational resources to bridge the gap between technical intricacies and user accessibility.

4. Potential for Misuse:

While Chain Keys enhance security, there is the potential for misuse if key management practices are not diligently followed. The compromise of private keys associated with Chain Keys can lead to unauthorized access and manipulation of cross-chain transactions. Educating users on secure key management practices and implementing robust security measures are essential to mitigate this risk.

5. Interoperability Challenges:

Achieving seamless interoperability between diverse blockchain networks using Chain Keys may pose challenges. The varying protocols, consensus mechanisms, and technical specifications of different blockchains may require additional considerations to ensure effective communication. Bridging the interoperability gap between blockchains with distinct characteristics is a hurdle that needs careful navigation.

Addressing the Cons and Future Directions:

Addressing the cons of Chain Keys involves a strategic approach to scalability, use case expansion, user education, and interoperability challenges. Future directions in the development and deployment of Chain Keys can focus on the following areas:

1. Scalability Solutions:

To overcome scalability challenges, ongoing research and development efforts can explore innovative solutions. Techniques such as sharding or hierarchical key structures may be investigated to optimize the management of Chain Keys as the number of interconnected blockchains grows. This ensures that the scalability of Chain Keys aligns with the increasing demand for cross-chain interoperability.

2. Use Case Diversification:

Expanding the use cases of Chain Keys involves identifying scenarios where trustless interaction is a critical requirement. Collaborative efforts between blockchain developers and industry stakeholders can explore new applications for Chain Keys, broadening their relevance beyond specific use cases. This diversification enhances the utility of Chain Keys in different cross-chain scenarios.

3. User-Friendly Interfaces:

To address the technical complexity associated with Chain Keys, the development of user-friendly interfaces is essential. Streamlining the user experience by designing intuitive interfaces and providing clear guidance on key management processes ensures broader accessibility. User education initiatives can bridge the gap between technical complexity and user-friendly interactions.

4. Robust Security Practices:

Mitigating the potential for misuse involves implementing and promoting robust security practices. This includes educating users on secure key management, implementing multi-factor authentication, and exploring advancements in cryptographic techniques to enhance the overall security posture of Chain Keys.

5. Interoperability Standards:

Enhancing interoperability involves the establishment and adoption of standards that facilitate seamless communication between different blockchain networks. Collaborative initiatives to define interoperability standards for Chain Keys can address compatibility challenges, fostering a more interconnected and interoperable blockchain ecosystem.

Conclusion:

The evaluation of the pros and cons of Chain Keys reveals a nuanced landscape where their strengths in trustless interaction, enhanced security, decentralization, privacy preservation, and real-world applications are counterbalanced by challenges related to scalability, limited use cases, technical complexity, potential misuse, and interoperability. Recognizing these aspects is crucial for steering the development and adoption of Chain Keys in a direction that maximizes their benefits while addressing inherent challenges.

As the blockchain industry continues to evolve, Chain Keys hold the potential to play a pivotal role in shaping the future of cross-chain interoperability. Strategic interventions, collaborative research, and a user-centric approach can collectively contribute to the refinement and optimization of Chain Keys, fostering a decentralized landscape where secure and trustless communication between blockchains becomes a fundamental reality.

Evaluating the Pros and Cons of Bridges

Bridges have emerged as instrumental components in addressing the challenges of interoperability within the blockchain ecosystem. This section conducts an in-depth evaluation of the advantages and disadvantages associated with the utilization of bridges for connecting diverse blockchain networks. By examining the inherent strengths and weaknesses, stakeholders can gain valuable insights into the practical implications of employing bridges for cross-chain communication.

Pros of Bridges:

Versatility:

Bridges offer a versatile solution that can be implemented in various forms, including smart contracts, dedicated networks, or specialized protocols. This adaptability allows bridges to cater to different blockchain ecosystems and use cases. Whether facilitating token swaps, cross-chain smart contracts, or decentralized identity management, the versatility of bridges enables them to address diverse interoperability needs.

Scalability:

Scalability is a critical consideration in the blockchain space, and bridges contribute significantly to addressing this challenge. By facilitating cross-chain transactions outside the main blockchain, bridges reduce congestion and enhance overall throughput. This off-chain processing capability ensures that interconnected blockchain networks can handle a higher volume of transactions without compromising efficiency.

Interoperability Standards:

Many bridges adhere to interoperability standards and protocols, providing a common framework for different blockchains to communicate. This standardization fosters a more seamless and efficient cross-chain ecosystem, allowing diverse blockchains to interoperate. Interoperability standards play a pivotal role in streamlining communication, reducing friction between different blockchain networks, and promoting a more interconnected blockchain landscape.

Consensus Flexibility:

Depending on the implementation, bridges can offer flexibility in choosing consensus mechanisms. This adaptability allows bridges to connect blockchains with varying consensus models, promoting compatibility. Whether interfacing with proof-of-work, proof-of-stake, or other consensus algorithms, bridges can act as bridges across different consensus landscapes, facilitating cross-chain communication.

Real-World Applications:

Bridges find practical applications in various real-world scenarios, showcasing their versatility and utility. One notable application is in facilitating interoperable token swaps, allowing users to exchange tokens between different blockchains seamlessly. Additionally, bridges play a crucial role in executing cross-chain smart contracts, extending the functionality of decentralized applications (DApps) to interact with multiple blockchains.

Cons of Bridges:

Centralization Risks:

One significant concern associated with certain bridge designs is the introduction of centralization risks. Centralized components or oracles within the bridge architecture could become potential points of failure, compromising the trustless nature of cross-chain transactions. Addressing centralization risks is essential to maintaining the integrity and security of bridges.

Security Vulnerabilities:

Bridges, especially those relying on smart contracts, are susceptible to security vulnerabilities. Flaws in smart contract code or vulnerabilities in the bridge architecture may be exploited by malicious actors, leading to potential security breaches. Ongoing security audits and best practices in smart contract development are crucial for mitigating these vulnerabilities.

Reliance on Trusted Oracles:

Certain bridge designs may rely on trusted oracles to relay information between blockchains. This introduces a level of reliance on external entities, and the compromise of trusted oracles could impact the overall security and trustlessness of the bridge. Implementing decentralized oracles or exploring alternative solutions to reduce reliance on trusted entities is essential for enhancing the robustness of bridges.

Privacy Concerns:

Depending on the implementation, bridges may face challenges in preserving user privacy. The relay of information between blockchains may expose transaction details, raising concerns about data confidentiality.

Implementing privacy-preserving solutions, such as zero-knowledge proofs or privacy-focused sidechains, becomes essential to address these privacy concerns.

Addressing the Cons and Future Directions:

Addressing the cons associated with bridges involves strategic interventions and ongoing research to mitigate centralization risks, enhance security, reduce reliance on trusted oracles, and address privacy concerns. Future directions in the development and deployment of bridges can focus on the following areas:

Decentralization Strategies:

To mitigate centralization risks, bridge designs can explore decentralization strategies. This may involve the use of decentralized oracles, distributed consensus mechanisms, or the implementation of protocols that minimize the reliance on centralized components. Ensuring that no single point of failure exists within the bridge architecture is crucial for preserving the trustless nature of cross-chain transactions.

Security Audits and Best Practices:

Addressing security vulnerabilities requires a proactive approach, including regular security audits and the adherence to best practices in smart contract development. Collaborating with security experts and engaging in thorough code reviews can help identify and rectify potential vulnerabilities, ensuring that bridges maintain a high level of security and resilience against malicious activities.

Decentralized Oracles:

Reducing reliance on trusted oracles involves exploring decentralized oracle solutions. Decentralized oracles distribute data retrieval and verification across a network of nodes, minimizing the risk associated with a single point of failure. Integrating decentralized oracles into bridge architectures enhances the overall security and trustlessness of cross-chain transactions.

Privacy-Preserving Solutions:

Addressing privacy concerns requires the implementation of privacy-preserving solutions within bridge designs. Techniques such as zero-knowledge proofs or privacy-focused sidechains can be employed to ensure the confidentiality of transaction details. Striking a balance between transparency and privacy is essential for fostering user trust and maintaining the integrity of cross-chain transactions.

Conclusion:

The evaluation of the pros and cons of bridges reveals a nuanced landscape where their versatility, scalability, adherence to interoperability standards, and consensus flexibility are counterbalanced by challenges related to centralization risks, security vulnerabilities, reliance on trusted oracles, and privacy concerns. Recognizing these aspects is crucial for steering the development and adoption of bridges in a direction that maximizes their benefits while addressing inherent challenges.

As the blockchain industry continues to evolve, bridges remain integral components in shaping the future of cross-chain interoperability. Strategic interventions, collaborative research, and a user-centric approach can collectively contribute to the refinement and optimization of bridges, fostering a decentralized landscape where secure and trustless communication between blockchains becomes a fundamental reality.

Matching the Approach to the Use Case

In the dynamic and diverse landscape of blockchain interoperability, selecting the most suitable approach is paramount. The choice between Chain Keys and Bridges, or a combination of both, depends on the specific requirements of the use case at hand. This section explores the nuanced process of matching the interoperability approach to the characteristics, needs, and goals of the use case, delving into considerations such as security, scalability, decentralization, and application domains.

Understanding Use Case Diversity:

The blockchain ecosystem is characterized by its diversity, with various platforms serving different purposes and industries. From decentralized finance (DeFi) applications and supply chain management to healthcare and identity verification, each use case presents unique challenges and opportunities. Understanding the intricacies of these diverse use cases is crucial for determining the most effective interoperability approach.

Security-Critical Use Cases:

In use cases where security is paramount, such as financial transactions and identity management, the choice of interoperability approach becomes critical. Chain Keys, with their emphasis on trustless interaction and cryptographic security, may be particularly well-suited for security-critical applications. The decentralized and cryptographic nature of Chain Keys enhances the integrity and confidentiality of transactions, mitigating the risks associated with unauthorized access and data manipulation.

Scalability Demands:

Scalability is a pressing concern in blockchain ecosystems, especially as user adoption and transaction volumes increase. Use cases with high scalability demands, such as decentralized exchanges and token swaps, may benefit from the scalability features offered by Bridges. The off-chain processing capabilities of Bridges alleviate congestion on the main blockchain, enabling a higher throughput of cross-chain transactions. Matching such scalability requirements with the appropriate interoperability approach is essential for ensuring the seamless and efficient execution of transactions.

Decentralization Requirements:

Certain use cases prioritize decentralization to eliminate single points of failure and enhance resilience. In applications where preserving the decentralized nature of blockchain technology is crucial, both Chain Keys and Bridges can play roles. Chain Keys contribute to decentralization by facilitating direct, trustless interaction between blockchains without relying on intermediaries. On the other hand, decentralized Bridge designs that minimize reliance on central entities or oracles also align with the decentralization requirements of certain use cases.

Industry-Specific Considerations:

Different industries have specific needs and regulatory considerations that influence the choice of interoperability approach. For instance, supply chain management may require a combination of Chain Keys and Bridges to ensure secure and transparent tracking of goods across multiple blockchain networks. Healthcare applications may prioritize privacy and data integrity, favoring Chain Keys with privacy-preserving features. Tailoring the interoperability approach to industry-specific requirements is crucial for successful implementation.

Use Case Examples:

Supply Chain Management:

In supply chain management, the need for transparency, traceability, and data integrity is paramount. Blockchain networks may represent various stakeholders within the supply chain, such as manufacturers, distributors, and retailers. Chain Keys can play a role in ensuring secure and trustless communication between these diverse blockchain networks. Additionally, Bridges may facilitate interoperable data exchange, allowing for real-time tracking of goods and transparent verification of the supply chain journey.

Decentralized Finance (DeFi):

The DeFi space, characterized by decentralized exchanges, lending platforms, and liquidity pools, demands a high level of security and scalability. Chain Keys can be employed to secure cross-chain transactions, ensuring that users can trade assets across different blockchain networks in a trustless manner. Simultaneously, Bridges contribute to scalability by processing transactions off-chain, reducing congestion on the main blockchain and enhancing the overall efficiency of decentralized financial applications.

Identity Verification:

Use cases involving identity verification and management require a delicate balance between privacy and security. Chain Keys, with their privacy-preserving features, can ensure that sensitive user information is not exposed during cross-chain identity verification processes. The decentralized nature of Chain Keys aligns with the principles of self-sovereign identity, empowering users with control over their personal information. Bridges may facilitate the seamless integration of identity data across multiple blockchain networks, ensuring a unified and interoperable identity management system.

Balancing Security and Usability:

The choice of interoperability approach involves a delicate balancing act between security and usability. While Chain Keys offer a trustless and secure model, their implementation may involve technical complexities that could impact user experience. Bridges, with their versatility and user-friendly interfaces, aim to bridge the usability gap but must ensure security and trustlessness. Striking the right balance is essential for achieving widespread adoption, especially in use cases where end-user interaction is crucial.

Addressing Regulatory Compliance:

Regulatory compliance is a critical consideration in many use cases, particularly as the blockchain industry navigates evolving legal frameworks. Matching the interoperability approach to regulatory requirements involves proactive engagement with regulatory authorities. Chain Keys, with their focus on trustless communication and security, can align with regulatory demands for data integrity and user protection. Bridges, designed with adherence to interoperability standards and privacy-preserving solutions, can facilitate compliance with regulatory frameworks.

Hybrid Approaches and Interoperability Standards:

In certain use cases, a hybrid approach that combines the strengths of both Chain Keys and Bridges may provide an optimal solution. This hybridization can address specific requirements that neither approach fulfills individually. Moreover, the development and adoption of interoperability standards become essential for ensuring compatibility and communication between diverse blockchain networks. Standards provide a common language and framework for interoperability, facilitating the matching of interoperability approaches to a wide array of use cases.

Challenges and Future Considerations:

Despite the strides made in matching interoperability approaches to use cases, challenges persist. Technical standardization, ongoing regulatory developments, and the dynamic nature of blockchain technologies present hurdles that require continuous attention. The future of interoperability will likely witness advancements in standardization efforts, further refinement of interoperability approaches, and increased collaboration between industry stakeholders, developers, and regulatory bodies.

Conclusion:

Matching the interoperability approach to the use case is a multifaceted process that demands a nuanced understanding of the specific requirements, challenges, and goals of diverse applications within the blockchain ecosystem. Whether addressing security-critical use cases, scalability demands, decentralization requirements, or industry-specific considerations, the careful selection of Chain Keys, Bridges, or hybrid approaches is crucial for successful implementation. As the blockchain industry continues to evolve, the adaptability and responsiveness of interoperability approaches to diverse use cases will play a pivotal role in shaping a more interconnected and efficient blockchain landscape.

Considering the Trade-offs between Security, Trustlessness, Scalability, and User Experience

In the pursuit of effective blockchain interoperability, stakeholders are confronted with intricate trade-offs between crucial factors: security, trustlessness, scalability, and user experience. This section delves into the nuanced considerations and balancing acts required when navigating these trade-offs, offering insights into the challenges and strategic decisions that define the landscape of interoperability solutions.

Security as the Cornerstone:

Security is a foundational consideration in any blockchain application, and interoperability solutions are no exception. The trust placed in blockchain networks stems from their ability to secure transactions and data. When considering the trade-offs, prioritizing security becomes paramount. Chain Keys, with their cryptographic underpinnings and focus on trustless interaction, are positioned as a secure solution. However, the challenge lies in ensuring that security is not compromised in the pursuit of other goals.

Trade-offs with Trustlessness:

Trustlessness is a defining characteristic of blockchain technology, emphasizing the elimination of reliance on central authorities. Achieving trustless interoperability is a core objective, especially when bridging different blockchain networks. Chain Keys contribute to trustlessness by facilitating direct communication without intermediaries. Yet, the challenge arises when trade-offs are required to accommodate scalability or user experience, potentially introducing elements that compromise the trustless model.

Navigating Scalability Challenges:

Scalability is an ongoing challenge in the blockchain space, and it is a critical consideration in the context of interoperability. While Chain Keys offer trustless interactions, they may face scalability challenges as the number of interconnected blockchains grows. Scaling trustless models requires innovative solutions to maintain security and decentralization. Scalability concerns are often at the forefront when evaluating trade-offs, as sacrificing scalability may hinder the broader adoption of interoperability solutions.

User Experience: Balancing Complexity and Accessibility:

User experience plays a pivotal role in the success of any technology. Blockchain interoperability, with its inherent complexities, must strike a delicate balance between technical sophistication and user-friendliness. Chain Keys, with their cryptographic nature, may introduce technical complexities that impact the overall user experience. Navigating these trade-offs involves designing intuitive interfaces, providing user education, and streamlining processes without compromising the security and trustless nature of the solution.

Strategic Considerations for Balancing Trade-offs:

Implementing Layered Security Measures:

To address the trade-offs between security and other factors, implementing layered security measures becomes crucial. This involves combining robust cryptographic techniques, secure key management practices, and regular security audits to fortify the interoperability solution. By layering security measures, stakeholders can enhance the overall resilience of the system without compromising other essential aspects.

Innovations in Scalability:

Innovative solutions are essential to overcoming scalability challenges while maintaining security and trustlessness. Research and development efforts should focus on scalability innovations, such as sharding, layer-2 solutions, and other scaling techniques. These innovations aim to optimize the performance of interoperability solutions, ensuring that they can scale seamlessly with the growing demands of interconnected blockchain networks.

Usability Enhancements:

Enhancing user experience involves a commitment to usability enhancements. This includes designing intuitive interfaces, creating comprehensive educational resources, and prioritizing user-friendly interactions. Striking a balance between complexity and accessibility requires continuous refinement based on user feedback and evolving technological capabilities. Usability enhancements should not compromise the security and trustless nature of the interoperability solution.

Hybrid Approaches:

Hybrid approaches that combine the strengths of different interoperability models can be strategic in mitigating trade-offs. For example, integrating both Chain

Keys and Bridges in a hybrid model may offer a balance between trustless communication and scalability. Hybrid approaches allow stakeholders to tailor solutions to specific use cases, leveraging the advantages of different interoperability components.

Real-world Applications and Trade-offs:

Decentralized Exchanges (DEXs):

In the context of decentralized exchanges, where security and trustlessness are paramount, the trade-offs become evident. Chain Keys can provide a secure and trustless environment for cross-chain asset swaps. However, scalability considerations may arise as transaction volumes increase. Balancing these trade-offs involves implementing scalable solutions, perhaps through layer-2 protocols, while maintaining the core principles of security and trustlessness.

Cross-Chain Token Swaps:

For applications involving cross-chain token swaps, the need for a seamless user experience is essential. Users engaging in token swaps expect simplicity and efficiency. Balancing this user-centric approach with the security and trustlessness provided by Chain Keys requires a thoughtful design that minimizes friction without compromising the integrity of the transaction.

Interoperable Smart Contracts:

In scenarios where interoperable smart contracts are central, considerations extend beyond individual transactions to the broader functionality of decentralized applications (DApps). The trade-offs involve optimizing smart contract execution for scalability without sacrificing security. Hybrid approaches that leverage both Chain Keys for secure communication and Bridges for scalability may be well-suited to address these multifaceted requirements.

Future Directions in Trade-off Resolution:

Advanced Cryptographic Techniques:

Advancements in cryptographic techniques can contribute to resolving trade-offs. Zero-knowledge proofs, homomorphic encryption, and other privacy-preserving cryptographic methods can enhance the security and privacy aspects of interoperability solutions. Implementing advanced cryptographic techniques allows stakeholders to navigate the trade-offs between security, scalability, and privacy more effectively.

Blockchain Governance and Standards:

The establishment of governance frameworks and interoperability standards is crucial for harmonizing diverse blockchain networks. By defining common protocols and communication standards, the industry can reduce friction in interoperability while adhering to security and trustlessness principles. Blockchain governance initiatives play a pivotal role in shaping the future landscape of interoperability and addressing trade-offs collaboratively.

Continuous Research and Innovation:

The dynamic nature of the blockchain industry necessitates continuous research and innovation. Solutions to existing trade-offs and challenges may emerge through breakthroughs in consensus algorithms, networking protocols, and system architectures. Research efforts focused on addressing the fundamental trade-offs will contribute to the evolution of interoperability solutions that align with the diverse needs of the blockchain ecosystem.

Conclusion:

Navigating the trade-offs between security, trustlessness, scalability, and user experience is a complex and ongoing challenge in the realm of blockchain interoperability. Stakeholders must make strategic decisions based on the specific requirements of their use cases, considering the diverse factors that contribute to the success of an interoperability solution. As the industry continues to advance, a commitment to innovation, collaboration, and a nuanced understanding of trade-offs will shape the development of interoperability solutions that strike a harmonious balance between security, trustlessness, scalability, and user experience.

Chapter 4: The Case for Trustless Interoperability
Making a Strong Case for the Trustless Paradigm

In the ever-evolving landscape of blockchain interoperability, the trustless paradigm stands out as a cornerstone principle that reshapes the way different blockchain networks communicate and transact. This section advocates for the trustless paradigm, delving into the fundamental concepts, security advantages, and transformative impact it brings to the broader blockchain ecosystem.

Understanding the Trustless Paradigm:

At its core, the trustless paradigm in blockchain refers to the ability of parties to interact and transact without requiring trust in intermediaries or central authorities. It embodies the decentralized ethos of blockchain technology, where cryptographic protocols and consensus mechanisms replace traditional trust-based relationships. Trustless interactions are a departure from traditional models that rely on centralized entities for validation and verification, ushering in a new era of autonomy, security, and resilience.

Security Advantages of Trustless Interoperability:

Eliminating Single Points of Failure:

One of the primary security advantages of the trustless paradigm is the elimination of single points of failure. In traditional centralized systems, a single compromised entity could jeopardize the entire network. Trustless interoperability, facilitated by technologies such as Chain Keys, ensures that there is no single entity holding the keys to cross-chain transactions. This decentralized approach enhances the overall security and resilience of the interconnected blockchain ecosystem.

Cryptography as a Security Pillar:

Trustless interoperability heavily relies on cryptographic techniques to secure transactions and communications between blockchain networks. The use of cryptographic keys, signatures, and hash functions ensures the confidentiality, integrity, and authenticity of data. Cryptography acts as a robust security pillar, providing a foundation for trustless interactions by making it computationally infeasible for malicious actors to compromise the security of the system.

Resilience to Attacks:

By distributing the validation and verification processes across a decentralized network, trustless interoperability enhances resilience to attacks. The absence of a single point of control makes it challenging for malicious actors to target and compromise the entire system. Even in the face of network nodes being compromised, the decentralized nature of trustless interoperability ensures that the overall integrity of the system remains intact.

The Pitfalls of Trust-Based Models:

To appreciate the significance of the trustless paradigm, it's crucial to understand the pitfalls associated with trust-based models in traditional systems.

Centralized Points of Control:

Traditional systems often rely on centralized points of control, where a single entity or a few intermediaries hold significant power. This concentration of control introduces vulnerabilities, as the compromise or manipulation of these central points can have cascading effects on the entire system.

Dependencies on Trusted Third Parties:

Trust-based models involve dependencies on trusted third parties, such as banks, clearinghouses, or centralized exchanges. Relying on these entities introduces counterparty risk, where users must trust that these intermediaries will act in their best interests. Trustless interoperability eliminates the need for such dependencies, reducing the risk of fraud, collusion, or unforeseen failures.

Lack of Transparency:

Trust-based models often lack transparency, making it challenging for users to verify the legitimacy of transactions or the overall health of the system. The trustless paradigm, with its emphasis on transparency through cryptographic verification, addresses this shortcoming, providing users with the ability to independently validate and audit transactions.

Building Trust in the Absence of Trust:

The paradox of the trustless paradigm lies in its ability to build trust in the absence of traditional trust relationships. It achieves this by leveraging cryptographic protocols and consensus mechanisms that provide verifiable and transparent assurances. Understanding how trust is established in trustless interoperability is crucial for making a compelling case for its adoption.

Decentralized Consensus Mechanisms:

Trustless interoperability relies on decentralized consensus mechanisms, such as proof-of-work or proof-of-stake, to validate transactions across interconnected blockchains. Through these mechanisms, consensus is achieved without the need for a central authority. The distributed nature of consensus ensures that no single entity can manipulate the validation process, fostering trust in the overall integrity of transactions.

Cryptography for Verifiable Transactions:

Cryptography plays a pivotal role in building trust by providing verifiable proof of the legitimacy and origin of transactions. Digital signatures, cryptographic hashes, and zero-knowledge proofs enable users to independently verify the authenticity of data without relying on trust in a centralized authority. This cryptographic assurance establishes a new paradigm of trust that is rooted in mathematical principles rather than institutional credibility.

Smart Contracts as Trust Executers:

Smart contracts, embedded in many blockchain networks facilitating trustless interoperability, serve as trust executors. These self-executing contracts automatically enforce predefined rules and conditions without requiring reliance on external parties. The deterministic nature of smart contracts ensures that the agreed-upon conditions will be executed as programmed, providing a trustless framework for executing transactions and agreements.

Real-World Applications of Trustless Interoperability:

Cross-Chain Asset Transfers:

Trustless interoperability finds practical application in facilitating cross-chain asset transfers. Users can securely and trustlessly transfer assets between different blockchain networks without relying on a central authority. The cryptographic verification ensures that the ownership and authenticity of the transferred assets are maintained, providing users with confidence in the security of cross-chain transactions.

Decentralized Exchanges (DEXs):

Decentralized exchanges leverage trustless interoperability to enable peer-to-peer trading of digital assets. Users can trade directly from their wallets without the need to deposit funds into a centralized exchange. The trustless nature of DEXs ensures that users maintain control over their assets throughout the trading process, mitigating the risk of exchange hacks or mismanagement.

Interoperable Smart Contracts:

Smart contracts that operate across multiple blockchain networks exemplify trustless interoperability in action. These contracts can execute complex logic and transactions seamlessly, interacting with different blockchains without relying on a centralized authority. This use case showcases the transformative potential of trustless interoperability in enabling new forms of decentralized applications and financial instruments.

Fostering Collaboration and Open-Source Development:

Trustless interoperability not only transforms the technical aspects of blockchain communication but also fosters collaboration and open-source development within the blockchain community.

Collaborative Development:

The trustless paradigm encourages collaborative development by removing barriers to entry and fostering an environment where developers can contribute to interoperability solutions without the need for centralized approvals. Open-source projects that embrace trustless interoperability benefit from a diverse pool of contributors, leading to rapid innovation and refinement of interoperability protocols.

Community Empowerment:

Trustless interoperability empowers the broader blockchain community by providing users and developers with tools to interact seamlessly across diverse blockchain networks. This empowerment reduces dependencies on centralized entities, promoting a more inclusive and decentralized ecosystem where participants have greater control over their digital assets and interactions.

Incentivizing Innovation:

The trustless paradigm incentivizes innovation by creating a level playing field for developers and entrepreneurs. With trustless interoperability, innovators can build applications and services that seamlessly interact with various blockchains, unlocking new possibilities for decentralized finance, supply chain management, and beyond. The elimination of gatekeepers and the reliance on trust-based models encourages bold experimentation and groundbreaking solutions.

Challenges and Considerations:

While the trustless paradigm brings transformative benefits, it is not without challenges and considerations that must be addressed for widespread adoption.

Scalability Concerns:

Achieving scalable trustless interoperability remains a challenge, especially as the number of interconnected blockchains grows. The decentralized consensus mechanisms that underpin trustless interoperability may face scalability constraints. Ongoing research and development efforts are necessary to address these concerns and ensure that trustless interoperability can scale effectively.

Usability and Education:

The cryptographic nature of trustless interoperability introduces complexities that can impact user experience. Usability challenges and the need for user education become critical considerations. Efforts to simplify interfaces, enhance educational resources, and streamline processes are essential to make trustless interoperability accessible to a broader audience.

Regulatory Considerations:

Regulatory frameworks, which are still evolving in the blockchain space, pose considerations for trustless interoperability. Navigating regulatory compliance while preserving the trustless nature of interactions is a delicate balance. Collaborative efforts between the blockchain industry and regulatory authorities are essential to establish frameworks that foster innovation while ensuring compliance.

Conclusion:

Making a strong case for the trustless paradigm in blockchain interoperability involves understanding its foundational principles, security advantages, and transformative impact on the broader blockchain ecosystem. Trustless interoperability shifts the narrative from dependence on centralized trust models to decentralized, cryptographic assurances. It empowers users, fosters collaboration, and incentivizes innovation, setting the stage for a more inclusive and resilient blockchain landscape. While challenges exist, ongoing research, collaboration, and a commitment to user-centric design will shape the future of trustless interoperability, unlocking new possibilities for decentralized applications and cross-chain interactions.

Eliminating Reliance on Trusted Third Parties

In the transformative landscape of blockchain technology, the concept of trustless interoperability represents a paradigm shift away from reliance on trusted third parties. This section explores the fundamental reasons behind eliminating dependence on intermediaries, the challenges posed by traditional trust models, and the profound impact of trustless interoperability on creating more resilient, secure, and user-centric blockchain ecosystems.

The Role of Trusted Third Parties in Traditional Systems:

In traditional systems, trusted third parties play a pivotal role in facilitating transactions, validating information, and ensuring the integrity of data. These entities, whether banks, clearinghouses, or centralized exchanges, act as intermediaries that users must trust to execute and verify transactions. The reliance on trusted third parties introduces several challenges that blockchain technology, specifically trustless interoperability, aims to overcome.

Counterparty Risk:

The concept of counterparty risk is inherent in systems that rely on trusted third parties. Users must trust that these intermediaries will act in their best interests, execute transactions accurately, and safeguard their assets. However, history has shown instances of financial crises, fraud, and failures of centralized entities, highlighting the vulnerability of trust-based models to counterparty risk.

Single Points of Failure:

Centralized intermediaries represent single points of failure in traditional systems. If a trusted third party is compromised, experiences a technical failure, or engages in malicious activities, the entire system may be at risk. The concentration of control in a few entities undermines the resilience and security of the overall ecosystem.

Lack of Transparency:

Traditional systems often lack transparency, making it challenging for users to verify the legitimacy of transactions or the actions of trusted third parties. Users are forced to trust that these intermediaries are acting ethically and in accordance with established rules. This lack of transparency diminishes accountability and exposes users to potential risks.

Trustless Interoperability as a Solution:

Trustless interoperability addresses these challenges by leveraging blockchain technology to eliminate the need for trusted third parties. The following key elements showcase how trustless interoperability transforms the landscape:

Decentralized Consensus:

Trustless interoperability relies on decentralized consensus mechanisms, such as proof-of-work or proof-of-stake, to validate and verify transactions across interconnected blockchain networks. This eliminates the need for a central authority to oversee or approve transactions, reducing counterparty risk and ensuring that consensus is achieved in a transparent and decentralized manner.

Cryptographic Verification:

The use of cryptographic techniques, such as digital signatures and cryptographic hashes, enables trustless verification of transactions. Participants in a trustless interoperability network can independently verify the authenticity and integrity of data without relying on a central authority. Cryptographic verification replaces the need for users to trust that a third party is executing transactions correctly.

Smart Contracts:

Smart contracts, integral to many blockchain networks facilitating trustless interoperability, serve as self-executing contracts that automatically enforce predefined rules and conditions. These contracts eliminate the need for intermediaries to oversee and execute transactions. Through code execution, smart contracts ensure that agreed-upon conditions are met without the need for trust in external parties.

Challenges of Traditional Trust Models:

Understanding the challenges posed by traditional trust models is crucial for appreciating the significance of eliminating reliance on trusted third parties through trustless interoperability.

Vulnerability to Hacks and Frauds:

Centralized entities storing user data or managing transactions become attractive targets for malicious actors seeking to exploit vulnerabilities. Hacks and frauds can compromise the security and privacy of user information, leading to financial losses and erosion of trust in the system. Trustless interoperability reduces this vulnerability by distributing control and minimizing the attractiveness of centralized targets.

Inefficiencies and Delays:

Traditional trust models often introduce inefficiencies and delays in transaction processes. Intermediaries, such as banks or clearinghouses, may require time to validate and settle transactions. Additionally, cross-border transactions may involve multiple intermediaries, leading to complex clearance procedures and delays. Trustless interoperability streamlines these processes, enabling faster and more efficient transactions without the need for intermediaries.

Costs and Fees:

Users engaging with trusted third parties incur costs and fees associated with transaction processing, verification, and other services. These costs contribute to the overall expenses borne by participants in traditional systems. Trustless interoperability, by eliminating intermediaries, reduces or eliminates such transaction costs, making transactions more cost-effective for users.

Building a Trustless Ecosystem:

Trustless interoperability contributes to the creation of a more resilient, secure, and user-centric blockchain ecosystem by addressing the challenges of traditional trust models.

Resilience through Decentralization:

Decentralization is a fundamental principle of trustless interoperability. By distributing control across a network of nodes, the system becomes more resilient to failures and attacks. The absence of a single point of control ensures that the ecosystem can withstand disruptions, providing users with increased confidence in the reliability of the network.

Enhanced Security through Cryptography:

The cryptographic foundation of trustless interoperability enhances security by providing verifiable proof of the legitimacy and origin of transactions. Users can independently verify the integrity of data through cryptographic signatures and hashes, reducing the risk of unauthorized access, manipulation, or fraudulent activities.

User Empowerment:

Trustless interoperability empowers users by enabling them to maintain control over their assets and transactions. Users are no longer reliant on trusted third parties to facilitate or verify transactions. This empowerment fosters a sense of autonomy and ownership, aligning with the principles of self-sovereign identity and financial independence.

Real-World Applications of Trustless Interoperability:

Cross-Border Transactions:

In the context of cross-border transactions, trustless interoperability facilitates seamless and secure transfers of value across different blockchain networks. Users can transact directly without the need for intermediaries, reducing costs, streamlining processes, and eliminating delays associated with traditional international transfers.

Supply Chain Management:

Trustless interoperability finds application in supply chain management, where multiple stakeholders across the supply chain interact and share information. Through decentralized consensus and cryptographic verification, trustless interoperability ensures the integrity and transparency of supply chain data. Participants can collaborate without relying on a central authority, reducing the risk of fraud and errors.

Decentralized Finance (DeFi):

Decentralized finance (DeFi) applications leverage trustless interoperability to create financial instruments and services without the need for traditional financial intermediaries. Users can trade, lend, and borrow assets directly from their wallets, benefiting from the security and transparency offered by trustless interoperability.

Overcoming Challenges:

While trustless interoperability offers significant advantages, challenges and considerations must be addressed for widespread adoption.

Scalability:

Achieving scalability in trustless interoperability networks is an ongoing challenge. The decentralized consensus mechanisms that ensure security may face scalability constraints as the number of interconnected blockchains grows. Research and development efforts focus on optimizing consensus algorithms and exploring layer-2 solutions to enhance scalability without compromising security.

Usability and Education:

The cryptographic nature of trustless interoperability introduces complexities that can impact user experience. Efforts to simplify interfaces, enhance educational resources, and streamline processes are essential to make trustless interoperability accessible to a broader audience.

Regulatory Considerations:

Navigating regulatory frameworks poses considerations for trustless interoperability. Collaborative efforts between the blockchain industry and regulatory authorities are essential to establish frameworks that foster innovation while ensuring compliance.

Conclusion:

Eliminating reliance on trusted third parties through trustless interoperability represents a foundational shift in the blockchain landscape. By addressing the vulnerabilities and challenges posed by traditional trust models, trustless interoperability contributes to the creation of a more resilient, secure, and user-centric ecosystem. The principles of decentralization, cryptographic verification, and user empowerment redefine how transactions are executed and verified, laying the groundwork for a trustless future in blockchain technology. As the industry continues to innovate and overcome challenges, trustless interoperability will play a pivotal role in shaping the next phase of blockchain evolution.

Addressing Potential Concerns Regarding Chain Keys

As blockchain technology advances and trustless interoperability becomes a focal point, Chain Keys emerge as a critical component. While Chain Keys offer innovative solutions for secure and trustless communication between blockchains, potential concerns and challenges must be addressed to ensure their widespread adoption. This section delves into these concerns, explores possible mitigations, and emphasizes the importance of continuous refinement and collaboration within the blockchain community.

Understanding Chain Keys in Trustless Interoperability:

Chain Keys serve as cryptographic keys that facilitate secure communication and interaction between different blockchain networks. They play a pivotal role in enabling trustless interoperability by allowing blockchain networks to verify the authenticity and integrity of transactions across disparate ledgers. As with any emerging technology, Chain Keys come with their set of challenges and concerns that necessitate careful consideration.

Potential Concerns:

Complexity and Technical Barrier:

One of the primary concerns surrounding Chain Keys is the perceived complexity and technical barrier for users and developers. The intricate cryptographic processes involved in generating, managing, and validating Chain Keys may pose challenges for those unfamiliar with advanced cryptographic concepts. This complexity could hinder the adoption of trustless interoperability solutions based on Chain Keys, particularly among users who seek more straightforward interactions.

Scalability Challenges:

Scalability is a recurring concern in the blockchain space, and Chain Keys are not exempt from this challenge. As the number of interconnected blockchains and transactions grows, scalability concerns may arise. The cryptographic operations associated with Chain Keys could potentially become resource-intensive, impacting the efficiency and scalability of trustless interoperability solutions.

Key Management and Security Risks:

Effective key management is crucial for the security of Chain Keys. Concerns may arise regarding the secure storage, transmission, and backup of keys, especially in scenarios where users interact with multiple blockchain networks. The compromise of Chain Keys poses a significant security risk, potentially enabling malicious actors to manipulate transactions and compromise the integrity of cross-chain communication.

Usability and User Experience:

The cryptographic nature of Chain Keys introduces complexities that may impact the overall usability and user experience. Users accustomed to traditional systems may find the adoption of Chain Keys challenging. Striking a balance between robust security measures and a user-friendly interface is essential to ensure that the benefits of trustless interoperability are accessible to a broader audience.

Mitigating Concerns and Challenges:

Usability Enhancements:

Improving the usability of Chain Keys is crucial for addressing concerns related to complexity and user experience. User-friendly interfaces, intuitive key management tools, and comprehensive educational resources can contribute to making Chain Keys more accessible. Collaborative efforts within the blockchain community to design standardized user interfaces and best practices for Chain Key interactions will play a significant role in mitigating these concerns.

Scalability Solutions:

To address scalability challenges associated with Chain Keys, ongoing research and development efforts focus on optimizing cryptographic processes and exploring scalable solutions. Innovations such as layer-2 protocols and advancements in cryptographic algorithms aim to enhance the efficiency of Chain Key operations, ensuring that trustless interoperability remains scalable even as the number of interconnected blockchains grows.

Advanced Cryptographic Techniques:

Leveraging advanced cryptographic techniques can enhance the security of Chain Keys and mitigate risks associated with key management. Innovations such as threshold cryptography, homomorphic encryption, and secure multi-party computation offer potential solutions to key security concerns. Integrating these techniques into the design of trustless interoperability solutions can strengthen the overall security posture of Chain Keys.

Secure Key Management Practices:

Establishing secure key management practices is paramount for mitigating security risks associated with Chain Keys. Implementing hardware wallets, secure key storage solutions, and robust backup mechanisms can enhance the resilience of key management. Additionally, education and awareness campaigns within the blockchain community can promote best practices for secure key handling, reducing the likelihood of key-related vulnerabilities.

Real-World Applications and Case Studies:

Cross-Chain Asset Transfers:

In the context of cross-chain asset transfers, real-world applications of Chain Keys showcase their efficacy. Users can securely and trustlessly transfer assets between different blockchain networks using Chain Keys. Case studies highlighting successful implementations of cross-chain asset transfers provide valuable insights into the practical applications of Chain Keys in ensuring the security and integrity of transactions.

Decentralized Exchanges (DEXs):

Decentralized exchanges leverage Chain Keys to enable peer-to-peer trading of digital assets. Users can trade directly from their wallets without the need to deposit funds into a centralized exchange. Real-world applications of Chain Keys in decentralized exchanges demonstrate their role in securing cross-chain transactions and facilitating trustless trading environments.

Interoperable Smart Contracts:

Trustless interoperability solutions based on Chain Keys enable the execution of interoperable smart contracts across multiple blockchain networks. Real-world applications of interoperable smart contracts showcase the potential for Chain Keys to play a vital role in creating decentralized applications that operate seamlessly across disparate ledgers.

The Role of Open-Source Development:

Open-source development plays a pivotal role in addressing concerns and challenges associated with Chain Keys. The collaborative nature of the blockchain community allows developers to contribute to the refinement of Chain Key protocols, implementation of best practices, and development of standardized tools. Open-source initiatives focusing on Chain Key usability, security, and scalability contribute to the continuous improvement of trustless interoperability solutions.

Future Directions in Chain Key Technology:

Research and Innovation:

The dynamic nature of blockchain technology calls for continuous research and innovation in the realm of Chain Keys. Ongoing research efforts aim to address existing concerns and explore new possibilities. Innovations in cryptographic techniques, key management protocols, and scalability solutions will shape the future of Chain Key technology, making it more robust, secure, and accessible.

Standardization Efforts:

Standardization efforts within the blockchain community contribute to the maturation of Chain Key technology. Establishing common protocols, interfaces, and best practices for Chain Keys enhances interoperability between different blockchain networks. Collaborative standardization initiatives ensure that Chain Key implementations adhere to consistent and widely accepted principles.

Community Engagement and Education:

Community engagement and education are integral to the successful adoption of Chain Keys. Providing resources, workshops, and educational materials that focus on Chain Key technology enhances awareness and understanding within the blockchain community. Community-driven initiatives that promote knowledge sharing and skill development contribute to overcoming challenges related to Chain Key adoption.

Conclusion:

Addressing potential concerns regarding Chain Keys is essential for the successful integration of trustless interoperability solutions into the broader blockchain ecosystem. As a fundamental component of secure cross-chain communication, Chain Keys require ongoing refinement, collaboration, and innovation. Mitigating concerns related to complexity, scalability, security, and usability involves a multi-faceted approach that encompasses technological advancements, open-source development, real-world applications, and community engagement. By proactively addressing these concerns, the blockchain community can unlock the full potential of Chain Keys in shaping a trustless future for interoperable blockchain networks.

The Future of Trustless Interoperability and Its Impact on the Blockchain Ecosystem

As blockchain technology continues to evolve, trustless interoperability emerges as a key driver shaping the future of the blockchain ecosystem. This section explores the potential trajectories, advancements, and profound impacts that trustless interoperability is poised to bring. From addressing current challenges to unlocking new possibilities, the future of trustless interoperability promises transformative changes that will reverberate across the entire blockchain landscape.

Envisioning the Evolution of Trustless Interoperability:

Innovations in Chain Key Technology:

The evolution of trustless interoperability hinges on continuous innovations in Chain Key technology. Researchers and developers are actively exploring advanced cryptographic techniques, key management protocols, and scalability solutions to enhance the efficiency, security, and usability of Chain Keys. Future advancements may introduce breakthroughs that further streamline cross-chain communication and foster a more seamless user experience.

Integration of Layer-2 Solutions:

To address scalability concerns, the integration of layer-2 solutions represents a promising avenue for the future of trustless interoperability. Layer-2 solutions, such as state channels and sidechains, offer mechanisms to conduct off-chain transactions while preserving the security guarantees of the underlying blockchain. Integrating these solutions into trustless interoperability frameworks can significantly enhance scalability without compromising security.

Interoperability Standards and Frameworks:

The establishment of interoperability standards and frameworks will play a pivotal role in shaping the future landscape. Standardization efforts within the blockchain community aim to create common protocols and interfaces for interoperability. These standards facilitate seamless communication between different blockchain networks, fostering a more interconnected and collaborative ecosystem.

Impact on Decentralized Finance (DeFi):

Expanding DeFi Ecosystem:

Trustless interoperability is poised to have a profound impact on the decentralized finance (DeFi) ecosystem. As interoperable smart contracts and Chain Keys become more sophisticated, DeFi applications will expand beyond individual blockchains. Users will have the ability to access a broader range of financial services seamlessly, regardless of the underlying blockchain, unlocking new opportunities for decentralized lending, borrowing, and trading.

Cross-Chain Asset Management:

The future of trustless interoperability envisions cross-chain asset management solutions that allow users to manage and allocate their digital assets across multiple blockchains. Decentralized asset managers leveraging Chain Keys could dynamically rebalance portfolios, optimize yields, and capitalize on opportunities across diverse blockchain networks. This capability introduces a new dimension to asset management in the decentralized realm.

Real-World Implementations and Industry Adoption:

Enterprise Integration:

The future of trustless interoperability extends beyond the realm of public blockchains, reaching into enterprise solutions. Businesses exploring blockchain adoption will seek interoperable solutions that seamlessly integrate with existing systems. Trustless interoperability frameworks, backed by robust Chain Key technology, will play a crucial role in facilitating secure and transparent communication between private and public blockchain networks.

Supply Chain Traceability:

In industries such as supply chain management, trustless interoperability will enhance traceability and transparency. Different participants in a supply chain, each utilizing their preferred blockchain network, can securely and trustlessly share information through interoperable smart contracts. This innovation will reduce fraud, streamline logistics, and provide consumers with verifiable information about the origin and journey of products.

Challenges and Considerations for the Future:

Regulatory Frameworks:

As the future of trustless interoperability unfolds, regulatory frameworks will need to adapt to accommodate the evolving landscape. Establishing clear guidelines and standards for cross-chain transactions, Chain Key management, and interoperable smart contracts will provide legal certainty and foster a conducive environment for innovation.

Security and Privacy Concerns:

The continued emphasis on security will be paramount in the future development of trustless interoperability. Solutions addressing potential security and privacy concerns associated with Chain Keys, cryptographic techniques, and cross-chain communication will be essential. Ongoing research and collaborative efforts within the blockchain community will play a crucial role in enhancing the robustness of trustless interoperability.

Fostering Collaboration and Open-Source Development:

Community-Driven Innovation:

The future of trustless interoperability hinges on community-driven innovation and open-source development. Collaboration within the blockchain community will lead to the refinement of interoperability standards, the creation of interoperable smart contract libraries, and the development of user-friendly interfaces for Chain Key interactions. By fostering a collaborative environment, the blockchain community can collectively address challenges and propel trustless interoperability forward.

Interoperability Alliances:

Interoperability alliances and partnerships will play a pivotal role in shaping the future landscape. Blockchain projects, organizations, and industry consortia collaborating to establish interoperability standards and share best practices will accelerate the adoption of trustless interoperability. These alliances will facilitate knowledge exchange, interoperability testing, and the creation of interoperable solutions that span multiple blockchain networks.

The Societal Impact:

Financial Inclusion:

Trustless interoperability has the potential to contribute significantly to financial inclusion. As interoperable DeFi solutions become more accessible, individuals in regions with limited access to traditional financial services can participate in the global economy. Trustless cross-chain transactions can enable seamless remittances, lending, and investment opportunities for populations previously underserved by traditional financial systems.

Data Ownership and Privacy:

The future of trustless interoperability aligns with the principles of data ownership and privacy. Users, empowered by Chain Keys and decentralized identity solutions, gain greater control over their personal data. Interoperable smart contracts that operate across different blockchain networks can facilitate secure data sharing while ensuring that individuals retain ownership and control over their sensitive information.

Conclusion:

The future of trustless interoperability holds immense promise, heralding a new era of collaboration, innovation, and inclusivity in the blockchain ecosystem. As Chain Key technology evolves, scalability challenges are addressed, and interoperability standards mature, the impact on decentralized finance, enterprise integration, and societal inclusion will be profound. Continuous collaboration, open-source development, and a commitment to addressing challenges will be the driving forces that shape a future where trustless interoperability becomes a cornerstone of the blockchain revolution. As the journey unfolds, the blockchain community is poised to witness and contribute to the realization of a more interconnected, secure, and user-centric blockchain landscape.

Fostering Collaboration and Open-Source Development in Trustless Interoperability

The success and widespread adoption of trustless interoperability within the blockchain ecosystem are intricately tied to the principles of collaboration and open-source development. This section explores the essential role that collaborative efforts and open-source initiatives play in advancing trustless interoperability solutions, from the development of interoperable standards to the creation of interoperable smart contract libraries.

The Collaborative Nature of Blockchain Technology:

Blockchain technology has always been synonymous with collaboration and community-driven innovation. From the inception of Bitcoin as an open-source project to the proliferation of diverse blockchain networks, the collaborative nature of the blockchain community has been foundational. Trustless interoperability, as a frontier of blockchain evolution, embraces and extends this collaborative ethos.

Building Interoperability Standards:

Standardization Initiatives:

Interoperability standards serve as the bedrock for seamless communication between different blockchain networks. The collaborative creation of these standards involves the collective efforts of developers, researchers, and industry stakeholders. Standardization initiatives aim to define common protocols, interfaces, and best practices that enable interoperability.

Collaboration Across Blockchain Projects:

Fostering collaboration across diverse blockchain projects is crucial for the establishment of interoperability standards. Blockchain networks often operate in silos, each with its unique features and protocols. Collaborative efforts to bridge these gaps and create standardized communication protocols facilitate interoperability. Forums, working groups, and collaborative platforms serve as spaces for developers to engage in cross-project discussions and coordinate efforts toward interoperable solutions.

Open-Source Development in Trustless Interoperability:

The Power of Open Source:

Open-source development lies at the heart of trustless interoperability. Opening up source code to the community promotes transparency, accountability, and inclusivity. The collaborative nature of open-source projects allows developers worldwide to contribute, review, and improve code, accelerating the pace of innovation in trustless interoperability.

Decentralized Contributions:

Trustless interoperability projects often adopt decentralized models of development. This decentralization extends beyond the technology itself to decision-making processes, governance structures, and project roadmaps. Decentralized contributions ensure that no single entity controls the development trajectory, aligning with the principles of decentralization inherent in blockchain technology.

Key Elements of Collaborative Trustless Interoperability Development:

Community Engagement:

Community engagement is fundamental to collaborative trustless interoperability development. Developers, researchers, and enthusiasts from different backgrounds and expertise areas come together to contribute their insights and skills. Engaging the broader community fosters diversity of thought, accelerates problem-solving, and ensures that the resulting solutions meet a wide range of use cases.

Transparent Communication:

Transparent communication is a cornerstone of successful collaboration in trustless interoperability projects. Developers and contributors communicate openly about project goals, challenges, and progress. Transparent communication builds trust within the community, encourages participation, and enables contributors to align their efforts effectively.

Iterative Development:

Iterative development, often guided by the principles of agile methodology, characterizes collaborative efforts in trustless interoperability. Developers release incremental updates, gather feedback from the community, and iterate on the codebase. This iterative approach allows for rapid adaptation to changing requirements and ensures that the development process remains responsive to evolving industry needs.

Creating Interoperable Smart Contract Libraries:

Shared Libraries for Smart Contracts:

Interoperable smart contract libraries are foundational components of trustless interoperability. These libraries house pre-built, standardized smart contracts that can execute seamlessly across different blockchain networks. Collaboratively creating and maintaining these libraries simplifies the development process for dApps and blockchain projects, reducing the barrier to entry for developers aiming to achieve cross-chain functionality.

Standardized Smart Contract Interfaces:

Collaborative efforts in creating standardized smart contract interfaces contribute to the creation of interoperable smart contract libraries. Standardized interfaces ensure that smart contracts can communicate effectively with one another, regardless of the underlying blockchain. Developers can leverage these interfaces to build applications that seamlessly interact with diverse blockchain networks.

Challenges in Collaborative Trustless Interoperability Development:

Coordination Challenges:

Coordination challenges arise in large, decentralized development communities. Coordinating the efforts of developers scattered across the globe requires effective communication channels, clear project governance, and well-defined contribution processes. Collaborative tools, such as version control systems and project management platforms, help mitigate coordination challenges.

Balancing Decentralization and Governance:

Balancing decentralization with effective governance is an ongoing challenge. While decentralization is a core tenet of blockchain development, the need for decision-making structures and project leadership remains. Collaborative trustless interoperability development seeks to strike a balance that empowers contributors while maintaining clear project direction.

Real-World Examples of Collaborative Trustless Interoperability Development:

Polkadot and Substrate:

Polkadot, a multi-chain network, and Substrate, its modular blockchain framework, exemplify collaborative trustless interoperability development. Polkadot enables different blockchains to transfer messages and value in a trustless manner. Substrate, being open source, invites developers to contribute to the evolution of the framework, allowing for the creation of custom blockchains with interoperability features.

Cosmos Network:

The Cosmos Network is another notable example of collaborative trustless interoperability development. Cosmos facilitates inter-blockchain communication through the Inter-Blockchain Communication (IBC) protocol. The Cosmos community actively collaborates on the development of the protocol, ensuring its continuous improvement and alignment with industry standards.

The Role of Trustless Interoperability Alliances:

Forming Interoperability Alliances:

Interoperability alliances bring together blockchain projects, organizations, and industry players with a shared goal of advancing trustless interoperability. These alliances serve as platforms for collaborative discussions, knowledge sharing, and the establishment of interoperability standards. By forming alliances, stakeholders in the blockchain space can pool resources, leverage collective expertise, and drive the development of interoperable solutions.

Cross-Project Testing and Validation:

Interoperability alliances often engage in cross-project testing and validation exercises. These initiatives involve testing the interoperability of different blockchain networks and ensuring that they can communicate effectively. Cross-project testing helps identify potential issues, refine interoperability standards, and build confidence in the reliability of trustless interoperability solutions.

Educational Initiatives for Collaborative Trustless Interoperability Development:

Knowledge Sharing and Skill Development:

Educational initiatives play a vital role in fostering collaboration in trustless interoperability development. Workshops, webinars, and educational resources help disseminate knowledge about interoperability standards, Chain Key technology, and best practices. Skill development programs empower developers to contribute effectively to collaborative projects.

Developer Grants and Incentives:

Developer grants and incentives encourage active participation in collaborative trustless interoperability development. Projects often allocate funds to support developers contributing valuable code, documentation, or improvements. These incentives promote sustained engagement, attract new contributors, and recognize the importance of individual contributions to the collaborative ecosystem.

Conclusion:

Fostering collaboration and open-source development is indispensable for the advancement of trustless interoperability within the blockchain ecosystem. The collaborative nature of blockchain technology, with its emphasis on community-driven innovation, transparent communication, and decentralized contributions, propels the development of interoperable solutions. From creating interoperability standards to building smart contract libraries, collaborative efforts lay the foundation for a more interconnected, inclusive, and resilient blockchain landscape. As the blockchain community continues to collaborate, share knowledge, and refine interoperability solutions, the future promises a trustless ecosystem that seamlessly connects diverse blockchain networks, unlocking new possibilities for innovation and collaboration.

Chapter 5: Real-World Applications and the Future Landscape

Chain Keys in Practice: Showcasing Real-World Implementations

The theoretical concepts of trustless interoperability and Chain Keys come to life through real-world applications that demonstrate the practical value of these innovations. This section delves into actual use cases where Chain Keys are implemented, showcasing their impact on diverse industries, from finance to supply chain management. By exploring these real-world implementations, we gain insights into the challenges faced, the benefits realized, and the potential for Chain Keys to revolutionize how different blockchain networks interact.

Cross-Border Payments and Remittances:

One of the prominent real-world applications of Chain Keys is in cross-border payments and remittances. Traditional international transfers often involve multiple intermediaries, resulting in high fees and slow processing times. Implementing Chain Keys for trustless interoperability allows users to initiate cross-border transactions directly between different blockchain networks.

Implementation Scenario:

Imagine a scenario where a user in Country A wants to send funds to a recipient in Country B. Country A utilizes Blockchain Network X, while Country B operates on Blockchain Network Y. Chain Keys enable the secure transfer of digital assets between these networks without relying on traditional banking intermediaries.

Benefits:

1. Speed and Efficiency: Chain Keys facilitate near-instantaneous cross-border transactions, eliminating the delays associated with traditional banking systems.

2. Reduced Costs: Trustless interoperability through Chain Keys reduces the need for multiple intermediaries, leading to lower transaction fees for users.

3. Enhanced Security: Cryptographic verification ensures the integrity and authenticity of transactions, reducing the risk of fraud and unauthorized access.

4. Global Accessibility: Users on different blockchain networks can seamlessly participate in cross-border transactions, fostering financial inclusion.

Decentralized Exchanges (DEXs):

Decentralized exchanges leverage Chain Keys to create a trustless environment for peer-to-peer trading of digital assets. Users retain control of their private keys, and trades occur directly between participants without the need for a centralized intermediary.

Implementation Scenario:

In a decentralized exchange scenario, users on Blockchain Network A and Blockchain Network B can trade their digital assets without the assets leaving their wallets. Chain Keys facilitate the secure verification of assets on both networks, ensuring that trades are executed trustlessly.

Benefits:

1. User Control: Participants have full control over their private keys and funds, reducing the risk of centralized exchange hacks.

2. Censorship Resistance: Trustless interoperability enables trading without reliance on centralized entities, providing censorship-resistant access to financial markets.

3. Global Liquidity: Liquidity pools across different blockchain networks can be tapped into, creating a more robust and globally accessible trading environment.

4. Reduced Counterparty Risk: Transactions occur directly between users' wallets, minimizing counterparty risk and enhancing the overall security of trades.

Supply Chain Traceability:

Implementing Chain Keys in supply chain management enhances traceability, transparency, and efficiency. Chain Keys enable secure communication and data sharing between different participants in a supply chain, each utilizing its preferred blockchain network.

Implementation Scenario:

Consider a supply chain where manufacturers, distributors, and retailers operate on distinct blockchain networks. Chain Keys enable the creation of interoperable smart contracts that facilitate the secure sharing of data related to product origin, shipping, and delivery.

Benefits:

1. Transparent Provenance: Chain Keys ensure that information about the origin and journey of products is securely recorded and shared across the supply chain.

2. Reduced Fraud: Trustless interoperability reduces the risk of fraudulent activities within the supply chain by providing an immutable and transparent record of transactions.

3. Efficient Collaboration: Different entities in the supply chain can securely share data, reducing communication barriers and fostering efficient collaboration.

4. Consumer Confidence: Trustless interoperability enhances consumer trust by providing verifiable and tamper-proof information about the authenticity and quality of products.

Interoperable Smart Contracts for Trade Finance:

Chain Keys play a crucial role in enabling interoperable smart contracts for trade finance. This application enhances the efficiency and security of trade-related transactions, reducing the reliance on traditional paper-based processes.

Implementation Scenario:

In international trade, where multiple parties, including exporters, importers, and banks, are involved, Chain Keys facilitate the creation of interoperable smart contracts. These contracts automate and secure various aspects of the trade process, from order fulfillment to payment settlement.

Benefits:

1. Automated Processes: Interoperable smart contracts streamline trade processes, automating tasks such as documentation verification, customs clearance, and payment processing.

2. Reduced Delays: Trustless interoperability ensures that information is shared in real-time between involved parties, reducing delays caused by manual processes.

3. Immutable Record Keeping: The use of Chain Keys ensures that the data recorded in smart contracts is tamper-proof, providing a reliable and auditable record of trade transactions.

4. Improved Risk Management: Smart contracts, powered by Chain Keys, can incorporate predefined conditions and triggers, allowing for more effective risk management in trade finance.

Cross-Platform Gaming Assets:

In the gaming industry, Chain Keys offer a solution for the interoperability of in-game assets across different gaming platforms and blockchain networks. Players can securely trade, sell, or transfer their digital assets between games without relying on centralized intermediaries.

Implementation Scenario:

Consider a scenario where a player earns a rare in-game item on Blockchain Gaming Network X. With Chain Keys, the player can securely transfer this item to another player on Blockchain Gaming Network Y, ensuring the ownership and authenticity of the digital asset.

Benefits:

1. Player Ownership: Chain Keys empower players with true ownership of in-game assets, allowing them to trade or transfer assets across different gaming platforms.

2. Marketplace Interoperability: Gamers can participate in cross-platform marketplaces, creating a more extensive and interconnected gaming economy.

3. Reduced Fraud and Scams: Trustless interoperability through Chain Keys minimizes the risk of

fraud and scams in digital asset trading within the gaming ecosystem.

4. Increased Player Engagement: The ability to move assets seamlessly between games enhances player engagement and fosters a more dynamic gaming experience.

Challenges and Considerations in Real-World Implementations:

While the real-world implementations of Chain Keys bring numerous benefits, several challenges and considerations must be addressed:

1. Scalability: Ensuring that Chain Keys can handle a growing number of transactions and interactions across diverse blockchain networks is a significant challenge.

2. Regulatory Compliance: Adhering to diverse regulatory frameworks across different jurisdictions presents challenges for real-world implementations, especially in industries with strict regulatory oversight.

3. User Education: The complexity of Chain Keys and trustless interoperability requires extensive user education to ensure that participants can interact seamlessly with the technology.

4. Standardization: Achieving widespread adoption of Chain Keys requires standardization efforts to ensure compatibility and interoperability across different implementations.

Future Directions in Chain Key Implementations:

1. Integration with Layer-2 Solutions: Future implementations may explore the integration of Chain Keys

with layer-2 solutions to enhance scalability and reduce transaction costs.

2. Enhanced Privacy Solutions: Developments in privacy-focused technologies may influence future Chain Key implementations, ensuring that sensitive information remains confidential.

3. Industry-Specific Applications: Tailoring Chain Key implementations to specific industries, such as healthcare, energy, or education, could unlock new use cases and benefits.

4. Cross-Blockchain Collaboration: Future implementations may focus on fostering collaboration between disparate blockchain networks, promoting a more interconnected ecosystem.

Conclusion:

The real-world implementations of Chain Keys showcase the transformative potential of trustless interoperability across various industries. From cross-border payments to supply chain traceability, the use of Chain Keys enhances security, efficiency, and transparency. As these applications continue to evolve and address challenges, the future landscape holds promising opportunities for Chain Keys to redefine how blockchain networks interact, opening doors to unprecedented levels of connectivity and collaboration across the decentralized ecosystem.

The Impact of Chain Key Implementations on Interoperability

In the dynamic landscape of blockchain technology, Chain Keys stand out as a key enabler for achieving trustless interoperability between diverse blockchain networks. This section delves into the profound impact of Chain Key implementations on interoperability, exploring how they address existing challenges, foster collaboration, and shape the future of cross-chain communication.

Overcoming Interoperability Challenges:

Scalability:

Chain Keys play a pivotal role in addressing scalability challenges associated with interoperability. By enabling secure and efficient communication between blockchain networks, Chain Keys contribute to the scalability of cross-chain transactions. The cryptographic principles underlying Chain Keys ensure that as transaction volumes increase, the system remains resilient and capable of handling a growing number of interactions.

Reducing Latency:

One of the significant challenges in achieving seamless interoperability is reducing latency, ensuring that cross-chain transactions occur in near real-time. Chain Keys streamline the verification process, minimizing the time required for cryptographic validation. This reduction in latency enhances the overall speed and responsiveness of interoperable transactions, making them more practical for various applications.

Enhancing Security:

Security is paramount in the realm of interoperability, where different blockchain networks with varying security postures need to communicate. Chain Keys introduce a robust layer of cryptographic security, ensuring the integrity and authenticity of transactions. The decentralized nature of Chain Key implementations also mitigates the risk of single points of failure, enhancing the overall security of cross-chain interactions.

Facilitating Seamless Asset Transfers:

One of the most tangible impacts of Chain Key implementations is their role in facilitating seamless transfers of digital assets between different blockchain networks. Whether it's cryptocurrencies, non-fungible tokens (NFTs), or other digital representations of value, Chain Keys empower users to transfer and utilize assets trustlessly across disparate blockchain environments.

Cross-Border Transactions:

Chain Keys revolutionize cross-border transactions by enabling users to transfer digital assets directly between different blockchain networks. This has significant implications for international trade, remittances, and cross-border payments, as users can engage in secure and efficient transactions without relying on traditional financial intermediaries.

Decentralized Exchanges:

In decentralized exchanges (DEXs), Chain Keys are instrumental in creating a trustless environment for peer-to-peer trading. Users can trade digital assets directly from their wallets, leveraging the security and efficiency of Chain

Keys to ensure that trades are executed without the need for a centralized authority. This not only enhances user control but also contributes to the overall decentralization of the trading ecosystem.

Enabling Interoperable Smart Contracts:

Chain Keys serve as the cryptographic foundation for the implementation of interoperable smart contracts, revolutionizing how these self-executing contracts operate across different blockchain networks. The impact extends to various industries, including finance, supply chain management, and decentralized applications (dApps).

Trade Finance and Supply Chain:

Interoperable smart contracts powered by Chain Keys automate and secure various aspects of trade finance and supply chain processes. From order fulfillment to payment settlement, these contracts ensure that information is shared securely and transparently across different participants in the ecosystem. This has the potential to streamline international trade, reduce delays, and enhance overall efficiency in supply chain management.

Decentralized Applications (dApps):

The impact of Chain Keys on interoperable smart contracts is particularly notable in the realm of decentralized applications. Developers can leverage Chain Keys to create dApps that seamlessly interact with multiple blockchain networks. This opens up new possibilities for creating cross-platform applications, gaming experiences, and financial services that transcend the limitations of individual blockchains.

Enhancing Decentralization and Security:

Chain Key implementations contribute significantly to the overarching principles of decentralization and security in the blockchain space. They empower users with greater control over their digital assets, reduce reliance on centralized intermediaries, and enhance the overall security posture of cross-chain transactions.

User Control and Ownership:

Users leveraging Chain Keys maintain control and ownership of their private keys, the cryptographic entities that grant access to their digital assets. This principle aligns with the foundational tenets of blockchain technology, where decentralization and user empowerment are paramount. Chain Keys ensure that users have the autonomy to manage and transfer their assets trustlessly.

Reducing Counterparty Risk:

In traditional financial transactions, counterparty risk is a significant concern. The use of Chain Keys in cross-chain interactions minimizes this risk by enabling transactions directly between users' wallets. This reduces reliance on centralized entities, mitigating the potential for fraud, hacking, or other malicious activities associated with centralized intermediaries.

Fostering Collaboration and Interoperability Standards:

Chain Key implementations contribute to fostering collaboration within the blockchain community and the establishment of interoperability standards. This collaborative spirit is essential for the continued evolution and maturation of trustless interoperability.

Interoperability Alliances:

The impact of Chain Key implementations is amplified through the formation of interoperability alliances. These alliances bring together blockchain projects, organizations, and industry players with a shared goal of advancing trustless interoperability. By fostering collaboration, these alliances contribute to the development of interoperability standards, testing frameworks, and best practices.

Community-Driven Innovation:

The community-driven nature of blockchain development is accentuated by the impact of Chain Key implementations. Developers, researchers, and enthusiasts collaborate to refine and enhance Chain Key technology. The open-source nature of many Chain Key implementations encourages community-driven innovation, leading to the discovery of new use cases, optimization of existing protocols, and the creation of interoperable solutions.

Challenges and Considerations in Chain Key Implementations:

While the impact of Chain Key implementations on interoperability is substantial, several challenges and considerations warrant attention:

Regulatory Compliance:

As interoperability solutions gain traction, navigating diverse regulatory landscapes becomes a critical consideration. Ensuring that Chain Key implementations comply with existing regulations and legal frameworks is essential for widespread adoption.

Scalability:

The scalability of Chain Key implementations remains a challenge, especially as the demand for cross-chain transactions increases. Ongoing research and development efforts are necessary to address scalability concerns and ensure that Chain Keys can handle the growing volume of transactions across different blockchain networks.

User Education:

The complexity of Chain Keys and trustless interoperability requires comprehensive user education. Ensuring that users understand how to manage their private keys, initiate cross-chain transactions, and navigate interoperable environments is crucial for widespread adoption.

Standardization Efforts:

The absence of standardized protocols for Chain Key implementations poses challenges for interoperability. Standardization efforts are necessary to ensure compatibility and seamless communication between different implementations. These standards should cover key aspects, including cryptographic algorithms, key management, and transaction formats.

Future Directions in Chain Key Implementations:

The impact of Chain Key implementations on interoperability sets the stage for exciting future developments:

Integration with Layer-2 Solutions:

Future Chain Key implementations may explore integration with layer-2 solutions to enhance scalability and reduce transaction costs. By leveraging off-chain scaling solutions, Chain Keys could facilitate a higher throughput of cross-chain transactions.

Enhanced Privacy Solutions:

Advancements in privacy-focused technologies may influence future Chain Key implementations. Solutions that enhance the privacy and confidentiality of cross-chain transactions while preserving the trustless nature of interoperability are likely to be explored.

Industry-Specific Applications:

Tailoring Chain Key implementations to specific industries, such as healthcare, energy, or education, could unlock new use cases and benefits. Customized Chain Key solutions may cater to the unique requirements of different sectors, fostering specialized interoperability applications.

Cross-Blockchain Collaboration:

Future Chain Key implementations may focus on fostering collaboration between disparate blockchain networks. Initiatives that promote a more interconnected ecosystem, allowing for seamless communication and asset transfers between diverse blockchains, could redefine the landscape of decentralized collaboration.

Conclusion:

The impact of Chain Key implementations on interoperability is multi-faceted, influencing how blockchain networks communicate, collaborate, and evolve. By addressing scalability challenges, facilitating seamless asset transfers, enabling interoperable smart contracts, enhancing decentralization and security, and fostering collaboration, Chain Keys contribute significantly to the maturation of trustless interoperability. As the blockchain community continues to innovate and refine Chain Key technology, the future promises a more interconnected and collaborative decentralized ecosystem, where users can trustlessly interact across diverse blockchain networks, unlocking new possibilities for cross-chain applications and services.

Navigating the Challenges and Opportunities in the Evolving Blockchain Landscape

The rapid evolution of the blockchain landscape presents a myriad of challenges and opportunities for the implementation and adoption of innovative technologies such as Chain Keys. This section explores the dynamic nature of the blockchain ecosystem, delving into the obstacles faced and the potential opportunities that arise as trustless interoperability and Chain Keys continue to shape the future of decentralized systems.

Challenges in the Evolving Blockchain Landscape:

Regulatory Complexity:

The regulatory landscape surrounding blockchain technology remains a complex challenge. Different jurisdictions often have varying approaches to regulating blockchain projects, cryptocurrencies, and decentralized applications. Navigating this intricate web of regulations poses challenges for the widespread adoption of Chain Keys, particularly in applications that involve cross-border transactions and collaborations.

Interoperability Standards:

Despite the promise of interoperability, the lack of standardized protocols poses a significant challenge. Different blockchain networks may implement varying interoperability solutions, making it challenging for seamless communication between them. The absence of universally accepted standards can hinder the scalability and widespread adoption of Chain Keys.

Scalability Concerns:

Scalability is a perpetual challenge in the blockchain space, and the implementation of Chain Keys is no exception. As the demand for cross-chain transactions grows, ensuring that Chain Keys can handle increased transaction volumes while maintaining efficiency and low latency becomes crucial. Scalability concerns must be addressed to meet the evolving needs of a growing and interconnected blockchain ecosystem.

User Education and Adoption:

The intricacies of Chain Keys and trustless interoperability demand a certain level of technical understanding, creating a barrier for mainstream adoption. Educating users on how to manage private keys, initiate cross-chain transactions, and navigate interoperable environments is essential. Overcoming this educational hurdle is crucial for ensuring that users can confidently and securely participate in the evolving blockchain landscape.

Security and Privacy Challenges:

While Chain Keys enhance security in cross-chain transactions, ensuring the overall security and privacy of the evolving blockchain landscape remains an ongoing challenge. Threats such as quantum computing and evolving cryptographic vulnerabilities necessitate continuous research and development efforts to fortify the security protocols surrounding Chain Keys.

Opportunities in the Evolving Blockchain Landscape:

Interoperability Alliances:

The challenges in achieving interoperability have spurred the formation of interoperability alliances and collaborations. Blockchain projects, organizations, and industry players are increasingly joining forces to address interoperability challenges collectively. These alliances present an opportunity to establish interoperability standards, share best practices, and accelerate the development of Chain Key solutions that work seamlessly across diverse blockchain networks.

Regulatory Clarity and Collaboration:

The evolving blockchain landscape offers opportunities for increased regulatory clarity and collaboration. Engaging with regulatory bodies and fostering open communication can lead to the development of frameworks that support the implementation of Chain Keys. Regulatory collaboration can create an environment where innovative technologies like Chain Keys can thrive while ensuring compliance with existing legal frameworks.

Scalability Solutions:

The scalability challenges inherent in the blockchain space also present opportunities for innovation. Ongoing research into layer-2 scaling solutions, sharding, and other scalability-enhancing technologies can pave the way for more efficient and scalable implementations of Chain Keys. Collaboration between blockchain projects to implement and test these solutions can contribute to the broader scalability of trustless interoperability.

User-Friendly Interfaces:

Addressing the challenge of user education and adoption presents an opportunity to develop more user-friendly interfaces for Chain Keys and interoperability solutions. Streamlining the user experience, creating intuitive interfaces, and providing educational resources can significantly enhance user confidence and participation in the evolving blockchain landscape.

Privacy-Centric Solutions:

As the blockchain landscape matures, opportunities arise for the development of privacy-centric solutions that complement Chain Keys. Enhancing the privacy features of cross-chain transactions and ensuring the confidentiality of sensitive information can contribute to the broader adoption of trustless interoperability in applications that prioritize data privacy.

Balancing Innovation and Regulation:

One of the critical considerations in navigating the evolving blockchain landscape is striking a balance between innovation and regulation. While innovation drives the development of transformative technologies like Chain Keys, regulatory compliance ensures a stable and secure environment for users and businesses. Opportunities lie in proactive engagement with regulatory bodies, advocating for sensible regulations that foster innovation without compromising security and compliance.

Cross-Industry Collaboration:

The dynamic nature of the blockchain landscape presents opportunities for cross-industry collaboration. Blockchain technology is not confined to a single sector, and the interoperability facilitated by Chain Keys opens doors for collaborative efforts between industries. Collaborations between finance, healthcare, supply chain, and other sectors can lead to innovative use cases and accelerate the adoption of interoperable solutions.

Strategies for Overcoming Challenges:

Engagement with Regulatory Bodies:

To address regulatory challenges, proactive engagement with regulatory bodies is essential. Blockchain projects, industry associations, and stakeholders can work collaboratively with regulators to provide insights into the technology, advocate for reasonable regulations, and participate in the development of frameworks that support the implementation of Chain Keys.

Standardization Efforts:

Industry-wide standardization efforts play a crucial role in overcoming interoperability challenges. Collaborative initiatives to establish interoperability standards for Chain Keys can provide a common framework that facilitates communication between different blockchain networks. Participating in standardization efforts can enhance the compatibility and scalability of Chain Key implementations.

Community Education and Outreach:

To overcome user education challenges, comprehensive community education and outreach programs are necessary. Blockchain projects and organizations can invest in creating educational resources, tutorials, and user-friendly interfaces that demystify the complexities of Chain Keys. Empowering users with the knowledge and tools to navigate trustless interoperability is key to broader adoption.

Research and Development:

Continuous research and development efforts are crucial for addressing scalability, security, and privacy challenges. Blockchain projects and research institutions can invest in exploring new consensus mechanisms, cryptographic techniques, and scalability solutions. Ongoing innovation ensures that Chain Keys evolve to meet the demands of the dynamic blockchain landscape.

Conclusion:

Navigating the challenges and opportunities in the evolving blockchain landscape requires a strategic and collaborative approach. As Chain Keys and trustless interoperability become integral to the decentralized ecosystem, addressing regulatory complexities, enhancing scalability, ensuring security and privacy, and fostering user adoption are key considerations. The evolving landscape also presents opportunities for collaboration, standardization, and cross-industry partnerships that can drive the widespread adoption of Chain Keys, contributing to the realization of a more interconnected and innovative blockchain future.

Emerging Trends and Advancements in Chain Key Technology

As the blockchain ecosystem evolves, so does the technology that underpins trustless interoperability—Chain Keys. This section explores the cutting-edge trends and advancements in Chain Key technology, offering a glimpse into the future of decentralized systems. From quantum-resistant cryptography to innovative consensus mechanisms, these emerging trends shape the trajectory of Chain Key development, enhancing security, scalability, and the overall potential of cross-chain communication.

Quantum-Resistant Cryptography:

One of the foremost trends in Chain Key technology is the exploration of quantum-resistant cryptography. The advent of quantum computing poses a potential threat to existing cryptographic algorithms, including those used in Chain Keys. Quantum-resistant cryptography aims to develop algorithms that remain secure even in the face of quantum threats. This emerging trend ensures the long-term resilience and security of Chain Key implementations against the evolving landscape of quantum computing.

Quantum-Safe Signature Schemes:

Research in quantum-safe signature schemes is a critical aspect of quantum-resistant Chain Key technology. Signature schemes that resist attacks from quantum computers ensure the continued integrity and authenticity of transactions. Implementing these quantum-resistant signatures in Chain Keys safeguards users' assets against potential quantum threats, fostering a secure and future-proof blockchain ecosystem.

Post-Quantum Key Exchange Protocols:

Key exchange protocols are fundamental to the security of Chain Keys. Emerging trends focus on developing post-quantum key exchange protocols that can withstand attacks from quantum adversaries. These protocols play a crucial role in establishing secure communication channels between different blockchain networks, ensuring the confidentiality and privacy of cross-chain transactions.

Interoperability Standards and Protocols:

As the demand for interoperability grows, the development of standardized protocols becomes paramount. Emerging trends in Chain Key technology include the establishment of interoperability standards and protocols that facilitate seamless communication between diverse blockchain networks. These standards enhance the compatibility of Chain Keys, allowing them to function across various implementations and fostering a more interconnected decentralized ecosystem.

Cross-Chain Communication Protocols:

Innovative protocols for cross-chain communication are emerging as a trend in Chain Key development. These protocols define the rules and mechanisms for secure data exchange between different blockchain networks. They play a crucial role in ensuring the interoperability of Chain Keys, enabling users to trustlessly transfer assets and information across disparate blockchain environments.

Interoperability Testing Frameworks:

The establishment of interoperability testing frameworks is an essential trend in ensuring the reliability and functionality of Chain Keys. These frameworks provide a systematic approach to testing the interoperability of different implementations, helping developers identify and address potential issues. The development of such testing frameworks contributes to the creation of robust and standardized Chain Key solutions.

Enhanced Privacy Solutions:

Privacy is a growing concern in the blockchain space, and emerging trends in Chain Key technology focus on enhancing privacy solutions for cross-chain transactions. As users seek greater confidentiality in their interactions, advancements in privacy-centric Chain Keys aim to address these concerns while preserving the trustless nature of interoperability.

Confidential Transactions with Chain Keys:

One of the emerging trends is the integration of confidential transactions with Chain Keys. This involves implementing cryptographic techniques that obfuscate transaction details, ensuring that the amounts and participants involved in a transaction remain confidential. This trend enhances the privacy features of Chain Keys, making them more appealing for users who prioritize confidentiality.

Zero-Knowledge Proofs in Cross-Chain Transactions:

The use of zero-knowledge proofs is gaining prominence as an emerging trend in Chain Key technology. Zero-knowledge proofs allow users to prove the validity of a statement without revealing the underlying information. Integrating zero-knowledge proofs into Chain Key transactions enhances privacy by enabling participants to verify the correctness of transactions without disclosing sensitive details.

Cross-Blockchain Collaboration:

A notable trend in Chain Key technology is the promotion of cross-blockchain collaboration. This involves the development of protocols and frameworks that facilitate seamless communication and collaboration between different blockchain networks. The goal is to create an interconnected ecosystem where Chain Keys can operate across multiple blockchains, unlocking new possibilities for decentralized applications and services.

Cross-Blockchain Smart Contracts:

The advancement of cross-blockchain smart contracts is a key trend in Chain Key development. These smart contracts can execute logic and transactions that span multiple blockchain networks. The implementation of Chain Keys in cross-blockchain smart contracts ensures the secure and trustless execution of decentralized applications that operate across diverse blockchain environments.

Universal Asset Standards:

Emerging trends in Chain Key technology include the exploration of universal asset standards that transcend individual blockchain networks. These standards define common formats for representing digital assets, making it easier for Chain Keys to facilitate the transfer of assets across different blockchains. Universal asset standards contribute to the interoperability and fluidity of asset movement in the decentralized ecosystem.

Integration with Layer-2 Solutions:

Scalability remains a persistent challenge in blockchain networks, and emerging trends in Chain Key technology involve integration with layer-2 solutions. These solutions aim to enhance the scalability of blockchain networks by processing transactions off-chain while ensuring the security and trustlessness of Chain Keys.

State Channels and Chain Keys:

State channels are an emerging layer-2 solution that allows participants to conduct transactions off-chain while maintaining the security of on-chain settlement. Integrating Chain Keys with state channels enables users to engage in trustless cross-chain transactions with reduced latency and increased throughput. This trend contributes to the scalability of Chain Key implementations.

Sidechains and Cross-Chain Asset Transfers:

Sidechains, as layer-2 solutions, provide an avenue for Chain Keys to facilitate cross-chain asset transfers. By moving assets to a sidechain, users can transact with Chain Keys in a more scalable and efficient environment. This trend addresses scalability concerns by leveraging sidechain infrastructure for secure and rapid cross-chain interactions.

Decentralized Identity and Chain Keys:

The integration of decentralized identity solutions with Chain Keys is an emerging trend that enhances the security and user control in cross-chain transactions. Decentralized identity platforms enable users to manage their identities without relying on centralized authorities. When combined with Chain Keys, this trend ensures that users have complete control over their digital assets and identities across different blockchain networks.

Self-Sovereign Identity with Chain Keys:

The concept of self-sovereign identity aligns with the principles of decentralization, and emerging trends involve integrating self-sovereign identity solutions with Chain Keys. Users can use their Chain Keys to prove ownership and control over their digital identities, facilitating secure and privacy-preserving interactions in the decentralized ecosystem.

Decentralized Authentication with Chain Keys:

Decentralized authentication mechanisms, coupled with Chain Keys, enhance the security of cross-chain transactions. Users can use their Chain Keys to authenticate themselves and authorize transactions without relying on centralized authentication services. This trend contributes to the overall security and user-centric nature of trustless interoperability.

Conclusion:

The future of Chain Key technology is marked by exciting trends and advancements that promise to redefine the landscape of trustless interoperability. From quantum-resistant cryptography and interoperability standards to enhanced privacy solutions and integration with layer-2 solutions, these trends contribute to the security, scalability, and usability of Chain Keys. As the blockchain ecosystem continues to evolve, the ongoing development and implementation of these trends position Chain Keys at the forefront of innovation, shaping a future where decentralized systems seamlessly communicate, collaborate, and thrive.

Envisioning the Future of Interoperable Blockchain Ecosystems

The journey towards a more interconnected and collaborative blockchain future is guided by the vision of interoperability. This section explores the possibilities and implications of the future landscape shaped by Chain Keys and trustless interoperability. From transformative real-world applications to the evolution of decentralized governance, envisioning the future of interoperable blockchain ecosystems unveils a tapestry of innovation, inclusivity, and decentralized collaboration.

Transformative Real-World Applications:

In the envisioned future, real-world applications of trustless interoperability powered by Chain Keys permeate various industries, bringing about transformative changes in how we conduct business, exchange value, and interact in the digital realm.

Cross-Border Finance and Payments:

The future of interoperable blockchain ecosystems revolutionizes cross-border finance and payments. With Chain Keys facilitating seamless communication between disparate financial networks, international transactions become faster, more cost-effective, and secure. Users can transfer assets across borders without the need for traditional intermediaries, unlocking new opportunities for global economic inclusion.

Supply Chain Traceability and Transparency:

Interoperable blockchain ecosystems, enhanced by Chain Keys, redefine supply chain traceability and transparency. From the source of raw materials to the end consumer, every step of the supply chain becomes traceable and verifiable. Chain Keys ensure that information flows securely between different participants in the supply chain, fostering a new era of accountability and sustainability.

Decentralized Identity and Digital Credentials:

The future landscape envisions decentralized identity solutions seamlessly integrated with Chain Keys. Users have self-sovereign control over their digital identities, and digital credentials are securely and trustlessly exchanged across various platforms. This has profound implications for identity verification, access management, and the protection of personal data.

Interconnected Internet of Things (IoT):

As the Internet of Things (IoT) continues to expand, interoperable blockchain ecosystems powered by Chain Keys enable seamless communication and collaboration among IoT devices. From smart homes to industrial applications, IoT devices can securely exchange data and execute transactions on decentralized networks, unlocking new levels of efficiency and autonomy.

Evolution of Decentralized Finance (DeFi):

The future of interoperable blockchain ecosystems propels the evolution of decentralized finance, transcending the limitations of individual blockchains and ushering in a new era of open and inclusive financial services.

Cross-Chain Decentralized Exchanges (DEXs):

Interoperable blockchain ecosystems facilitate the development of cross-chain decentralized exchanges. Users can trade assets seamlessly across different blockchain networks, leveraging the security and trustlessness of Chain Keys. This evolution enhances liquidity, reduces reliance on centralized exchanges, and empowers users with greater control over their assets.

Liquidity Pools and Yield Farming Across Chains:

The envisioned future sees the creation of liquidity pools and yield farming opportunities that span multiple blockchains. Chain Keys enable the secure movement of assets between liquidity pools on different networks, fostering a more interconnected and efficient decentralized financial ecosystem. Users can participate in yield farming strategies that transcend individual blockchain silos.

Interoperable Lending and Borrowing Protocols:

Decentralized lending and borrowing protocols evolve into interoperable systems. Users can access lending and borrowing services across different blockchain networks, with Chain Keys ensuring the secure and transparent execution of smart contracts. This opens up avenues for cross-chain collateralization and diversified lending strategies.

Decentralized Autonomous Organizations (DAOs) and Governance:

The future landscape envisions the maturation of decentralized governance structures, where interoperability facilitated by Chain Keys enhances collaboration and decision-making across DAOs.

Cross-DAO Collaboration and Voting:

Interoperable blockchain ecosystems enable cross-DAO collaboration and voting. DAOs from different networks can collaborate on shared initiatives, pooling resources and expertise. Chain Keys secure the voting mechanisms, ensuring that decisions are made transparently and trustlessly across disparate decentralized organizations.

Decentralized Cross-Chain Governance Platforms:

Emerging as a trend in decentralized governance, cross-chain governance platforms become integral to the future landscape. These platforms, supported by Chain Keys, provide a standardized framework for governance processes that span multiple blockchains. This fosters a more cohesive and collaborative approach to decision-making in the decentralized ecosystem.

Decentralized Identity in Governance:

Decentralized identity, empowered by Chain Keys, plays a crucial role in governance structures. DAO members can securely establish and prove their identities using Chain Keys, enhancing the integrity of decision-making processes. This trend contributes to the development of more inclusive and accountable decentralized governance models.

Inclusive Token Economies and Cross-Chain Token Transfers:

The future of interoperable blockchain ecosystems envisions token economies that transcend individual networks, allowing for seamless cross-chain token transfers and fostering a more inclusive digital economy.

Interconnected Token Ecosystems:

Blockchain projects issue tokens that seamlessly exist and operate across multiple networks. Chain Keys facilitate the secure transfer of these tokens, enabling users to engage with diverse token economies without the need for complex and centralized exchanges. This trend encourages collaboration between projects and a more inclusive digital asset ecosystem.

Cross-Chain NFT Marketplaces:

Non-fungible tokens (NFTs) become a cornerstone of interoperable blockchain ecosystems. Chain Keys enable secure cross-chain transfers of NFTs, unlocking new possibilities for artists, collectors, and enthusiasts. Cross-chain NFT marketplaces emerge, allowing users to explore, trade, and showcase their digital assets on a global scale.

Decentralized Cross-Chain Token Bridges:

Interoperable blockchain ecosystems feature decentralized cross-chain token bridges. These bridges, supported by Chain Keys, facilitate the secure and trustless movement of tokens between different blockchain networks. This evolution eliminates the need for centralized intermediaries, enhancing the efficiency and security of cross-chain token transfers.

Enhanced Security and Privacy Features:

The future landscape of interoperable blockchain ecosystems emphasizes continuous advancements in security and privacy features, ensuring the integrity of cross-chain transactions and user data.

Zero-Knowledge Proofs and Chain Keys:

Zero-knowledge proofs become a standard feature in interoperable blockchain ecosystems. Chain Keys, combined with zero-knowledge proofs, enhance the privacy of cross-chain transactions by allowing users to prove the validity of transactions without revealing sensitive information. This evolution contributes to a more confidential and secure decentralized ecosystem.

Quantum-Resistant Chain Keys:

As quantum computing advances, the future of interoperable blockchain ecosystems prioritizes the integration of quantum-resistant Chain Keys. These cryptographic keys withstand the potential threats posed by quantum adversaries, ensuring the long-term security of cross-chain transactions and user assets.

Privacy-Focused Cross-Chain Smart Contracts:

Interoperable blockchain ecosystems feature privacy-focused cross-chain smart contracts. Users can execute complex and confidential transactions across different blockchains, leveraging Chain Keys to ensure the security and privacy of the contract logic. This trend enhances the versatility and privacy features of decentralized applications.

Global Collaboration and Open-Source Development:

The envisioned future embraces a culture of global collaboration and open-source development, where interoperable blockchain ecosystems supported by Chain Keys foster innovation and inclusivity.

Cross-Chain Developer Communities:

Interoperable blockchain ecosystems nurture cross-chain developer communities. Developers from different networks collaborate on shared protocols, standards, and solutions. Chain Keys secure the development process, ensuring that open-source contributions are transparent and trustworthy across diverse blockchain environments.

Shared Interoperability Standards:

The future landscape sees the establishment of shared interoperability standards that transcend individual blockchain networks. These standards, collaboratively developed and maintained by the global blockchain community, ensure a consistent and secure framework for Chain Keys and trustless interoperability. This evolution contributes to the seamless interaction between diverse decentralized systems.

Global Initiatives for Interoperability Research:

Interoperability research becomes a global initiative, with academic institutions, industry leaders, and blockchain projects collaborating on cutting-edge advancements. Chain Keys, as a fundamental component of interoperability, are continuously refined and enhanced through collaborative research efforts. This trend accelerates the development of secure and scalable solutions for trustless interoperability.

Conclusion:

The future of interoperable blockchain ecosystems, guided by the transformative power of Chain Keys, holds a promise of innovation, collaboration, and inclusivity. From real-world applications that revolutionize finance and supply chain to the evolution of decentralized finance and governance, the envisioned landscape reflects a harmonious and interconnected decentralized ecosystem. As security features advance, token economies become more inclusive, and global collaboration thrives, Chain Keys emerge as the linchpin of trustless interoperability, shaping a future where blockchain technology transcends boundaries, empowers individuals, and redefines the way we interact with decentralized systems.

Conclusion

The Key Takeaways: A Reiteration of Chain Keys' Advantages

In concluding our exploration of blockchain interoperability, with a specific focus on Chain Keys and trustless models, it is essential to reiterate and underscore the profound advantages that Chain Keys bring to the table. Throughout this journey, we have delved into the dawn of interoperability, navigated roadblocks, and unveiled the path to trustless interoperability. We have explored the world of Chain Keys, scrutinized the architecture of blockchain bridges, conducted a comparative analysis of interoperability approaches, made a compelling case for trustless paradigms, and glimpsed into real-world applications and the future landscape. As we distill the essence of our exploration, let's reiterate the key takeaways that highlight the unique advantages of Chain Keys.

1. Trustless Communication as the Essence:

At the heart of the advantages offered by Chain Keys lies the essence of trustless communication. Unlike traditional models that rely on centralized intermediaries or trusted third parties, Chain Keys empower users with the ability to engage in secure, verifiable, and direct communication across different blockchain networks. Trustless communication ensures that participants can transact and interact without compromising the decentralization principles that underpin blockchain technology.

2. Unparalleled Security Features:

Security is paramount in the blockchain space, and Chain Keys emerge as a robust solution to fortify the security of cross-chain transactions. The use of cryptographic techniques, including public and private key pairs, ensures that only authorized parties can initiate and validate transactions. Furthermore, the incorporation of quantum-resistant cryptography addresses potential future threats, safeguarding the integrity and confidentiality of data exchanged through Chain Keys.

3. Mitigating the Pitfalls of Trustless Interoperability:

While trustless interoperability is a groundbreaking paradigm, it is not without challenges. Chain Keys, however, serve as a mitigating force against these pitfalls. By providing a secure and decentralized means of communication, Chain Keys alleviate concerns related to fraud, double-spending, and unauthorized access. The careful design and implementation of Chain Keys contribute to the overall resilience and reliability of trustless interoperability.

4. Maturity and Future Advancements in Chain Key Technology:

Evaluating the maturity of Chain Key technology reveals its current standing in the blockchain landscape. As of now, Chain Keys demonstrate a level of sophistication that enables secure cross-chain transactions. Yet, the journey doesn't end here. The continuous exploration of future advancements in Chain Key design remains a critical aspect. This commitment to innovation ensures that Chain Keys evolve to meet the dynamic needs of an ever-changing blockchain ecosystem, embracing scalability, efficiency, and adaptability.

5. Bridging the Gaps with Blockchain Bridges:

In the realm of interoperability, blockchain bridges play a pivotal role. Chain Keys, integrated with these bridges, offer a seamless connection between otherwise siloed blockchain networks. The architectural design of bridges, coupled with the security features of Chain Keys, addresses the challenges associated with cross-chain communication. This holistic approach fosters a unified blockchain future, where diverse networks collaborate without compromising security or decentralization.

6. A Comprehensive Comparative Analysis:

The comparative analysis of Chain Keys versus bridges underscores the nuanced considerations that influence the choice of interoperability approach. Chain Keys, with their focus on trustless communication, stand out for their security advantages. However, a comprehensive understanding requires an evaluation of the pros and cons of both Chain Keys and bridges. This comparative analysis serves as a guide for matching the interoperability approach to specific use cases, considering the trade-offs between security, trustlessness, scalability, and user experience.

7. Case for Trustless Interoperability:

Making a strong case for trustless interoperability emerges as a pivotal theme. Chain Keys, as a key enabler of trustlessness, eliminate the reliance on trusted third parties, presenting a paradigm shift in how blockchain networks interact. The advantages of trustless interoperability extend beyond security to encompass the fundamental principles of decentralization, empowering users to transact without intermediaries and fostering a more inclusive and equitable digital economy.

8. Addressing Concerns and Fostering Collaboration:

Chain Keys address potential concerns associated with their implementation, including issues related to security, user education, and regulatory considerations. By providing solutions to these challenges, Chain Keys pave the way for a future where trustless interoperability becomes not only a reality but also a catalyst for collaboration and open-source development. The emphasis on fostering collaboration within the blockchain community contributes to the collective advancement of Chain Keys and trustless interoperability.

9. Real-World Implementations Showcase Viability:

The exploration of real-world applications demonstrates the practical viability of Chain Keys. Showcasing their implementation in scenarios such as cross-border finance, supply chain traceability, decentralized identity, and interconnected IoT devices validates the advantages of trustless interoperability. Real-world use cases underscore the transformative impact of Chain Keys in diverse industries, substantiating their role in shaping the future of decentralized systems.

10. Envisioning a Future of Interconnected Ecosystems:

As we cast our gaze into the future, we envision a landscape where interoperable blockchain ecosystems seamlessly collaborate, driven by the transformative power of Chain Keys. This vision encompasses the evolution of decentralized finance, the maturation of decentralized governance, the inclusivity of token economies, enhanced security and privacy features, and a global culture of collaboration and open-source development. Chain Keys emerge as the linchpin that propels blockchain technology beyond current limitations, fostering a future where decentralized systems are interconnected, collaborative, and capable of reshaping the digital landscape.

In conclusion, the key takeaways reaffirm that Chain Keys are not merely a technological component but a foundational element that reshapes how blockchain networks interact. As we embark on this journey towards a unified blockchain future, the advantages of Chain Keys stand as pillars supporting the vision of trustless interoperability. The evolution of this technology, coupled with a commitment to security, collaboration, and innovation, positions Chain Keys as catalysts for a decentralized revolution that transcends boundaries and empowers individuals globally.

The Significance of Interoperability in the Growth of Blockchain Technology

In the concluding chapter of our exploration into the intricate world of blockchain interoperability, it is imperative to underscore the profound significance of this concept in the overall growth and maturation of blockchain technology. Interoperability, especially when fueled by innovations like Chain Keys, represents more than just a technical advancement; it embodies a paradigm shift that has far-reaching implications for the entire blockchain ecosystem. As we unravel the layers of significance, we delve into the impact on scalability, adoption, collaboration, and the very fabric of decentralization that defines blockchain technology.

Unleashing Scalability Beyond Silos:

Scalability has been a persistent challenge for blockchain networks since their inception. Interoperability, driven by mechanisms like Chain Keys, emerges as a solution that transcends the siloed nature of individual blockchains. Rather than being confined to the limitations of a single network, blockchain scalability is unleashed across interconnected ecosystems. Chain Keys facilitate the secure and trustless communication necessary for the seamless flow of data and value between disparate blockchains, unlocking a new era of scalability for decentralized applications and services.

The significance lies not only in accommodating growing transaction volumes but also in providing a framework for sustained growth without compromising the fundamental tenets of decentralization. As Chain Keys become integral to interoperability, the scalability bottleneck that has hindered widespread blockchain adoption begins to loosen its grip, paving the way for a more robust and globally scalable blockchain infrastructure.

Driving Adoption Through Seamless User Experience:

Interoperability, when seamlessly integrated with user-centric solutions like Chain Keys, becomes a catalyst for blockchain adoption. One of the persistent barriers to the widespread acceptance of blockchain technology has been the complexity and fragmentation of the ecosystem. Users often encounter challenges when navigating between different blockchains, each with its unique architecture, tokens, and functionalities.

Chain Keys, as enablers of trustless interoperability, address this challenge by providing a unified experience for users. The significance lies in creating an environment where users can interact with various blockchain networks effortlessly, leveraging the benefits of decentralized applications and services without being impeded by technical complexities. This enhanced user experience becomes a driving force behind the mass adoption of blockchain technology, extending its reach to individuals and industries that previously found the technology inaccessible.

Fostering Collaboration and Cross-Chain Innovation:

Interoperability is not merely about connecting blockchains; it is about fostering a culture of collaboration and cross-chain innovation. The significance of this collaborative ethos becomes evident as blockchain networks, enabled by Chain Keys, engage in shared initiatives, research, and open-source development. Rather than existing as isolated entities, blockchains become nodes in a vast, interconnected network where ideas, protocols, and solutions flow seamlessly.

Chain Keys play a pivotal role in securing this collaborative ecosystem. Their trustless nature ensures that participants can engage in cross-chain initiatives without compromising security or relying on centralized authorities. The significance lies in the potential for accelerated innovation, where advancements made in one blockchain network can catalyze progress across the entire interconnected landscape. The shared knowledge and resources enabled by Chain Keys propel the blockchain community into a new era of collective growth and exploration.

Preserving Decentralization Amidst Connectivity:

A core tenet of blockchain technology is decentralization—an ethos that underpins trust, security, and user empowerment. The significance of interoperability, especially when considering the role of Chain Keys, is in preserving and enhancing decentralization amidst increasing connectivity. As blockchain networks become more interconnected, the challenge is to maintain the principles of decentralization that make blockchain technology resilient and censorship-resistant.

Chain Keys, through their trustless communication model, ensure that the interconnected nature of blockchains does not compromise decentralization. The security advantages they provide, combined with cryptographic principles, create a foundation where users can trustlessly transact and interact without relying on centralized intermediaries. This significance is pivotal in ensuring that as blockchain networks grow and interconnect, they remain true to the principles that have been at the core of the technology's appeal.

Empowering a Global and Inclusive Digital Economy:

Interoperability, with Chain Keys at its forefront, plays a pivotal role in reshaping the dynamics of the global digital economy. The significance lies in the empowerment of individuals and communities across the globe. As blockchain networks seamlessly communicate, individuals gain access to a borderless and inclusive financial ecosystem. Trustless interoperability ensures that financial transactions can occur across borders without the need for traditional intermediaries, reducing costs and fostering financial inclusion.

Chain Keys become the keys to financial autonomy, enabling users to securely manage their assets and participate in a decentralized global economy. The significance extends beyond financial transactions to encompass decentralized identity, supply chain traceability, and various real-world applications that empower individuals with control over their data and assets.

Safeguarding Security and Privacy in an Interconnected World:

In an era of increasing connectivity, the significance of Chain Keys and interoperability is evident in the safeguarding of security and privacy. As blockchain networks interconnect, the potential for data breaches, fraud, and unauthorized access increases. Chain Keys, by providing a trustless means of communication, mitigate these risks, ensuring that sensitive information remains secure even in a highly interconnected blockchain landscape.

The cryptographic principles embedded in Chain Keys, including zero-knowledge proofs and quantum-resistant cryptography, contribute to a more secure and private decentralized ecosystem. The significance lies in establishing a robust foundation for trustless interoperability, where users can transact and share data with confidence, knowing that their security and privacy are prioritized.

Catalyzing the Evolution of Decentralized Finance (DeFi):

The decentralized finance (DeFi) revolution has been a driving force in the blockchain space, and the significance of Chain Keys in interoperability is particularly pronounced in the evolution of DeFi. As DeFi protocols and services span multiple blockchains, Chain Keys enable the seamless movement of assets and data between these networks. This interconnected DeFi landscape, secured by trustless communication, brings new dimensions to financial services.

The significance lies in the creation of a truly decentralized and interoperable financial ecosystem. Users can access diverse DeFi services, including decentralized exchanges, lending platforms, and liquidity pools, without being confined to a single blockchain network. Chain Keys, as the linchpin of trustless interoperability, catalyze the evolution of DeFi, making it more accessible, efficient, and inclusive.

Paving the Way for a Unified Blockchain Future:

Ultimately, the significance of interoperability with Chain Keys lies in its role as the architect of a unified blockchain future. As blockchain networks evolve from isolated entities to interconnected ecosystems, the vision is one of collaboration, innovation, and inclusivity. Chain Keys, with their trustless communication model, are the keys that unlock this unified future, where diverse networks seamlessly communicate and collaborate without sacrificing security or decentralization.

The significance is in the creation of a blockchain landscape that transcends current limitations, where users can seamlessly navigate between different networks, where decentralized applications can leverage the strengths of multiple blockchains, and where the principles of trustlessness and decentralization are upheld across a globally connected ecosystem. Chain Keys, in their role as enablers of trustless interoperability, pave the way for a future where blockchain technology realizes its full potential, fostering a digital revolution that reshapes industries, empowers individuals, and transcends borders.

Conclusion:

In conclusion, the significance of interoperability, particularly when driven by innovations like Chain Keys, cannot be overstated. It represents the key to unlocking the next phase of blockchain evolution—a phase where scalability, adoption, collaboration, decentralization, and global empowerment converge. As we reflect on the journey through the intricacies of interoperability, it becomes evident that Chain Keys are not just a technological component; they are the catalysts that propel blockchain technology into a new era. Their significance lies in shaping a future where blockchain networks seamlessly communicate, collaborate, and coalesce into a unified force that transforms the digital landscape.

A Call to Action: Exploring and Contributing to the Advancement of Trustless Interoperability

As we conclude our deep dive into the intricacies of blockchain interoperability, guided by the transformative power of Chain Keys, it is crucial to issue a resounding call to action. The exploration has taken us through the dawn of interoperability, the roadblocks hindering seamless communication, the unveiling of the path to trustless interoperability, and a comprehensive examination of Chain Keys' role in shaping the future. Now, as we stand at the intersection of theory and practice, it is time to turn our attention to the active role each stakeholder in the blockchain community can play in advancing the cause of trustless interoperability.

The Imperative of Continuous Exploration:

Interoperability, particularly the trustless variety powered by Chain Keys, is not a static concept; it is a dynamic force that evolves alongside the blockchain landscape. The call to action begins with a commitment to continuous exploration. Stakeholders—developers, researchers, industry leaders, and enthusiasts—are urged to stay abreast of the latest advancements in Chain Key technology and interoperability protocols.

Engaging in continuous learning, attending conferences, and participating in community discussions are essential components of this exploration. By staying informed and curious, individuals contribute to the collective knowledge base that propels the field forward. The imperative is not just to understand the current state of trustless interoperability but to actively contribute to its evolution by pushing boundaries and envisioning new possibilities.

Empowering Developers to Embrace Trustless Interoperability:

Developers stand at the forefront of innovation, and the call to action for this group is to embrace and integrate trustless interoperability into their projects. Whether building decentralized applications, smart contracts, or blockchain infrastructure, developers have the power to infuse Chain Keys into the very fabric of their creations.

This empowerment requires a dual commitment—to adopt existing interoperability solutions that leverage Chain Keys and to contribute to the development of new tools and frameworks. Open-source collaboration becomes a cornerstone, as developers across different projects join forces to create interoperability standards that seamlessly integrate Chain Keys. The call is not just to write code but to architect a future where blockchain applications can communicate across networks, fostering a decentralized ecosystem that transcends silos.

Forging Partnerships for Cross-Chain Initiatives:

The call to action extends to industry leaders, blockchain projects, and institutions to forge partnerships for cross-chain initiatives. The significance of trustless interoperability lies not just in its technical prowess but in the collaborative networks it facilitates. Blockchain networks, each with its strengths and use cases, can achieve more when they collaborate.

Establishing cross-chain collaborations requires a mindset shift from competition to cooperation. Industry leaders can lead by example, demonstrating the value of interoperable solutions powered by Chain Keys. This can involve joint research efforts, the establishment of interoperability standards, and the creation of shared resources. By forming alliances, the blockchain industry can amplify its collective impact, advancing the adoption and sophistication of trustless interoperability.

Investing in Education and User Awareness:

Education is a key driver of adoption, and the call to action emphasizes the need for widespread education and user awareness initiatives. Users, both within and outside the blockchain space, need to understand the significance of trustless interoperability and Chain Keys. This involves demystifying technical concepts, explaining the benefits, and addressing common misconceptions.

Educational initiatives can take various forms—online courses, workshops, webinars, and educational content tailored for different audiences. The goal is to empower users with the knowledge to make informed decisions about adopting interoperable solutions powered by Chain Keys. As awareness spreads, the user base grows, contributing to the organic expansion of trustless interoperability across the blockchain ecosystem.

Regulatory Engagement for a Supportive Environment:

A crucial aspect of the call to action is engaging with regulators to foster a supportive environment for trustless interoperability. Regulatory clarity is essential for the widespread adoption of blockchain technology, and this clarity becomes even more critical when it comes to interoperability across different networks.

Blockchain industry leaders, legal experts, and advocacy groups can play a pivotal role in engaging with regulators to articulate the benefits of trustless interoperability. By contributing to the development of regulatory frameworks that encourage innovation while ensuring security and compliance, stakeholders can create an environment where Chain Keys and interoperable solutions can flourish.

Supporting Interoperability Research and Development:

The call to action extends to academia, research institutions, and blockchain projects to actively support interoperability research and development. Trustless interoperability is a field ripe for exploration and innovation. Researchers can delve into the intricacies of Chain Keys, exploring novel cryptographic techniques, security enhancements, and scalability solutions.

Academic institutions can establish interdisciplinary research programs focused on blockchain interoperability, attracting top talent to contribute to the field. Simultaneously, blockchain projects can allocate resources and collaborate with research institutions to sponsor research initiatives. The goal is to push the boundaries of what is possible, uncovering new avenues for advancing trustless interoperability and the role of Chain Keys in shaping the future.

Community Engagement and Grassroots Advocacy:

The strength of the blockchain community lies in its decentralized and grassroots nature. The call to action encourages individuals at every level—enthusiasts, developers, and advocates—to actively engage with their communities and become grassroots advocates for trustless interoperability.

This engagement can take the form of organizing meetups, participating in online forums, contributing to open-source projects, and educating peers about the benefits of Chain Keys. Grassroots advocacy builds a groundswell of support, fostering a community-driven movement that propels trustless interoperability into the mainstream.

Incorporating Feedback and Iterating Solutions:

Trustless interoperability is a journey, and the call to action emphasizes the importance of incorporating feedback and iterating on solutions. The blockchain space is dynamic, with user needs and technological challenges evolving over time. Developers, industry leaders, and users must actively participate in providing feedback on interoperability solutions.

This feedback loop is essential for refining Chain Keys, interoperability protocols, and associated tools. It ensures that solutions are not just technically sound but also responsive to the needs of the user community. The call is not just to create solutions but to foster a culture of continuous improvement, where every iteration brings the ecosystem closer to the vision of seamless, trustless interoperability.

Conclusion:

In conclusion, the call to action is a rallying cry for active participation in the advancement of trustless interoperability, with Chain Keys at its core. It is a call for exploration, collaboration, education, advocacy, and continuous improvement. Each stakeholder—developers, industry leaders, researchers, educators, advocates, and users—has a unique role to play in shaping the future of blockchain technology.

Trustless interoperability is not a distant goal; it is a reality that can be collectively built and refined. The call is not just to envision a future where blockchain networks seamlessly communicate but to actively contribute to making that vision a reality. As we embark on this collective journey, guided by the transformative power of Chain Keys, the call to action becomes a shared commitment to a decentralized future that transcends barriers, empowers individuals, and redefines the way we interact with blockchain technology.

The Role of Chain Keys in Shaping the Future of a Unified Blockchain Landscape

As we navigate the intricate terrain of blockchain technology and its quest for interoperability, the spotlight turns to the pivotal role of Chain Keys in sculpting the future of a unified blockchain landscape. These cryptographic keys represent more than just a technical mechanism; they are the linchpin that holds the promise of creating seamless connections, breaking down silos, and fostering a decentralized ecosystem where diverse blockchain networks collaborate harmoniously. In this exploration, we delve into the multifaceted role that Chain Keys play in shaping the future of interoperability.

Empowering Trustless Connections:

At the core of Chain Keys' role is the empowerment of trustless connections across disparate blockchain networks. Traditional modes of interaction often rely on trusted intermediaries or centralized entities to facilitate communication. However, Chain Keys introduce a paradigm shift by enabling direct and secure communication without the need for intermediaries. The cryptographic keys, working in tandem with advanced cryptographic techniques, lay the foundation for a trustless environment where parties can transact and interact with confidence.

In shaping the future, this role becomes increasingly significant. Trustless connections, facilitated by Chain Keys, not only enhance security but also align with the fundamental principles of decentralization—a cornerstone of blockchain technology. As the ecosystem evolves, the ability to establish trustless connections becomes a catalyst for the development of decentralized applications, cross-chain transactions, and innovative use cases that transcend the limitations of individual blockchains.

Mitigating Interoperability Roadblocks:

Interoperability, while a beacon for the future, is not without its challenges. Chain Keys emerge as a formidable solution to mitigate these roadblocks. The complexities associated with cross-chain communication, security vulnerabilities, and the risk of fraud find a counterbalance in the cryptographic principles embedded in Chain Keys.

The role of Chain Keys in overcoming these challenges extends beyond mere functionality. It represents a commitment to creating an interoperable environment that is both robust and secure. As the blockchain landscape continues to expand and diversify, the ability of Chain Keys to navigate these challenges becomes instrumental in ensuring that interoperability is not a theoretical concept but a practical and reliable mechanism for blockchain networks to communicate seamlessly.

Facilitating Cross-Chain Transactions:

A unified blockchain landscape envisions a future where cross-chain transactions are not only feasible but also efficient and secure. Chain Keys serve as the digital passports that enable assets to traverse different blockchain networks. The cryptographic signatures and secure communication channels established by Chain Keys validate transactions, ensuring that they adhere to the rules and consensus mechanisms of the participating blockchains.

In shaping this facet of the future, Chain Keys contribute to the maturation of decentralized finance (DeFi), cross-border finance, and various industries that rely on the seamless transfer of assets. The role of Chain Keys extends to creating an environment where users can effortlessly move value between different blockchain networks, unlocking new possibilities for financial innovation, inclusivity, and global collaboration.

Enhancing Security in a Connected Ecosystem:

Security remains a paramount concern in the blockchain space, especially as networks become more interconnected. The role of Chain Keys in shaping the future is intricately linked to enhancing the security posture of the entire ecosystem. By employing cryptographic techniques such as public and private key pairs, digital signatures, and zero-knowledge proofs, Chain Keys fortify the integrity of transactions and the confidentiality of sensitive information.

As blockchain networks evolve into a connected ecosystem, the ability of Chain Keys to provide a secure and verifiable means of communication becomes indispensable. Their role extends to safeguarding against potential threats, including double-spending attacks, unauthorized access, and data breaches. Chain Keys become the guardians of trustless communication, instilling confidence in users and fostering a secure environment for blockchain interactions.

Fostering a Culture of Decentralization:

Decentralization is the beating heart of blockchain technology, and the role of Chain Keys aligns seamlessly with this ethos. As blockchain networks seek to collaborate and communicate without reliance on central authorities, Chain Keys become the embodiment of a decentralized approach to trust and security.

In shaping the future, the role of Chain Keys extends beyond technical functionality to fostering a culture of decentralization. Their implementation signifies a commitment to principles that prioritize user autonomy, censorship resistance, and the elimination of single points of failure. Chain Keys become instrumental in ensuring that as blockchain networks unite, they do so in a manner that upholds the foundational values that have driven the adoption and growth of decentralized systems.

Enabling Cross-Industry Collaboration:

The future of blockchain technology is not confined to a single industry or use case; it is a tapestry woven by the collaboration of diverse sectors. Chain Keys play a vital role in enabling cross-industry collaboration by providing a standardized and secure means of communication. Whether it's healthcare, supply chain, finance, or identity management, the role of Chain Keys extends to creating an interoperable fabric that transcends industry silos.

This cross-industry collaboration facilitated by Chain Keys sparks innovation and creates synergies that go beyond the capabilities of individual blockchain networks. The role of Chain Keys in shaping the future lies in their ability to act as bridges, connecting disparate industries and unlocking the potential for new applications and services that can revolutionize how information and value are exchanged.

Paving the Way for Mass Adoption:

The journey toward a unified blockchain landscape is incomplete without addressing the imperative of mass adoption. Chain Keys, by virtue of their role in enabling seamless, trustless interactions, play a pivotal role in paving the way for mass adoption. As users experience the benefits of interoperability—whether through cross-chain transactions, decentralized applications, or enhanced security—they are more likely to embrace blockchain technology on a broader scale.

In shaping the future, the role of Chain Keys in driving mass adoption becomes a linchpin for the entire ecosystem. Their user-friendly implementation and the elimination of technical complexities contribute to a more accessible and inclusive blockchain environment. The role of Chain Keys extends to becoming catalysts for a paradigm shift where blockchain technology becomes a ubiquitous and integral part of everyday life.

Fulfilling the Vision of a Unified Blockchain Future:

Ultimately, the role of Chain Keys in shaping the future is about fulfilling the vision of a unified blockchain landscape. This vision transcends the individual capabilities of blockchain networks, envisioning an interconnected ecosystem where trustless communication is the norm. Chain Keys become the instruments that orchestrate this vision, ensuring that the future of blockchain technology is not fragmented but unified.

As the role of Chain Keys unfolds, it becomes evident that they are not just tools; they are architects of a new era. An era where blockchain networks collaborate seamlessly, where users experience the benefits of decentralized applications without friction, and where the principles of trustless communication redefine the digital landscape. The role of Chain Keys is to serve as the catalysts that propel the entire blockchain ecosystem into this future—a future where unity, trustlessness, and decentralization converge to reshape how we perceive and interact with technology.

THE END

Glossary

Here are some key terms and definitions related to AI-driven cryptocurrency investing:

1. Blockchain Interoperability: The capacity of diverse blockchain networks to interact seamlessly, allowing the exchange of data and transactions across different platforms.

2. Chain Keys: Cryptographic keys that play a crucial role in enabling trustless communication and secure interactions between blockchain networks.

3. Trustless Model: A decentralized approach where interactions and transactions occur without the need for trust in third parties, relying instead on cryptographic verification and consensus mechanisms.

4. Bridges: Connective mechanisms or protocols that facilitate interoperability between distinct blockchain networks, allowing the transfer of assets and data.

5. Decentralized Finance (DeFi): A financial ecosystem built on blockchain technology that aims to recreate and enhance traditional financial services without reliance on central authorities.

6. Oracles: External entities or services that provide real-world data to smart contracts on the blockchain, enabling them to execute based on real-world events.

7. Relayers: Agents or nodes responsible for transmitting information between different blockchain networks, often associated with bridge-based interoperability.

8. Zero-Knowledge Proofs: Cryptographic techniques that allow a party to prove the authenticity of information

without revealing the actual data, enhancing privacy and security.

9. Quantum-Resistant Cryptography: Cryptographic algorithms designed to withstand attacks from quantum computers, ensuring the long-term security of blockchain systems.

10. Decentralized Applications (DApps): Applications built on blockchain networks that operate without a central authority, leveraging smart contracts and decentralized protocols.

11. Cross-Chain Transactions: Transactions that involve the transfer of assets or data between different blockchain networks, facilitated by interoperability solutions such as Chain Keys.

12. Smart Contracts: Self-executing contracts with the terms of the agreement directly written into code, automating and enforcing contractual agreements on the blockchain.

13. Cryptography: The practice and study of techniques for securing communication and data through the use of mathematical algorithms, foundational to blockchain security.

14. Security Tokens: Digital tokens representing ownership or rights to an underlying asset, often subject to regulatory compliance and security measures.

15. Cross-Industry Collaboration: Collaboration and integration of blockchain technology across various industries to create synergies and foster innovation.

16. Mass Adoption: The widespread acceptance and use of blockchain technology and associated applications by the general public and mainstream industries.

17. Decentralization: The distribution of authority and control across a network rather than being concentrated in a single entity, a fundamental principle of blockchain technology.

18. Interoperability Standards: Agreed-upon protocols and specifications that facilitate seamless communication and interaction between different blockchain networks.

19. Digital Identity: A digital representation of an individual or entity that can be used for authentication and authorization purposes in the digital realm.

20. Open-Source Development: Software development approach where the source code is made available to the public, encouraging collaboration, transparency, and community contribution.

Potential References

In addition to the content presented in this book, we have compiled a list of supplementary materials that can provide further insights and information on the topics covered. These resources include books, articles, websites, and other materials that were used as references throughout the writing process. We encourage you to explore these materials to deepen your understanding and continue your learning journey. Below is a list of the supplementary materials organized by chapter/topic for your convenience.

Introduction:

Antonopoulos, A. M. (2014). "Mastering Bitcoin: Unlocking Digital Cryptocurrencies." O'Reilly Media.

Narayanan, A., et al. (2016). "Bitcoin and Cryptocurrency Technologies: A Comprehensive Introduction." Princeton University Press.

Mougayar, W. (2016). "The Business Blockchain: Promise, Practice, and Application of the Next Internet Technology." John Wiley & Sons.

Chapter 1: Delving into the World of Chain Keys:

Boneh, D., et al. (2001). "Identity-based encryption from the Weil pairing." Advances in Cryptology—CRYPTO 2001.

Katz, J., & Lindell, Y. (2007). "Introduction to Modern Cryptography." Chapman and Hall/CRC.

Buterin, V. (2013). "Ethereum: A Next-Generation Smart Contract and Decentralized Application Platform."

Chapter 2: Bridges: Bridging the Gaps between Blockchains:

Wood, G. (2014). "Ethereum: A Secure Decentralised Generalised Transaction Ledger." Ethereum Project Yellow Paper.

Back, A. (2014). "Enabling Blockchain Innovations with Pegged Sidechains." Blockstream Whitepaper.

Swan, M. (2015). "Blockchain: blueprint for a new economy." O'Reilly Media.

Chapter 3: A Comparative Analysis of Interoperability Approaches:

Zohar, A. (2015). "Bitcoin: under the hood." Communications of the ACM, 58(9), 104-113.

Todd, P., et al. (2016). "Segregated witness benefits."

King, S., & Nadal, S. (2012). "PPCoin: Peer-to-Peer Crypto-Currency with Proof-of-Stake." PPCoin Whitepaper.

Chapter 4: The Case for Trustless Interoperability:

Szabo, N. (1997). "Formalizing and securing relationships on public networks." First Monday, 2(9).

Micali, S. (2016). "Algorand: The Efficient and Democratic Ledger." arXiv preprint arXiv:1607.01341.

Narayanan, A., et al. (2016). "Bitcoin and Cryptocurrency Technologies: A Comprehensive Introduction." Princeton University Press.

Chapter 5: Real-World Applications and the Future Landscape:

Tapscott, D., & Tapscott, A. (2016). "Blockchain revolution: how the technology behind bitcoin is changing money, business, and the world." Penguin.

Swan, M. (2018). "Blockchain: blueprint for a new economy." O'Reilly Media.

Mougayar, W. (2016). "The Business Blockchain: Promise, Practice, and Application of the Next Internet Technology." John Wiley & Sons.

Conclusion:

Narayanan, A., et al. (2016). "Bitcoin and Cryptocurrency Technologies: A Comprehensive Introduction." Princeton University Press.

Tapscott, D., & Tapscott, A. (2016). "Blockchain revolution: how the technology behind bitcoin is changing money, business, and the world." Penguin.

Swan, M. (2018). "Blockchain: blueprint for a new economy." O'Reilly Media.

www.ingramcontent.com/pod-product-compliance
Lightning Source LLC
LaVergne TN
LVHW012041070526
838202LV00056B/5555